RESEARCH REPORTS
REFEREEING PROCESS

The Research Committee considers it is essential to apply a rigorous refereeing process to all stages of its research reports. The refereeing process operates by sending the proposal to two independent referees (one academic and one practitioner), who thereafter remain in close contact with the project and are further consulted on the academic and technical standard of the eventual publication.

PANEL OF ACADEMIC REFEREES

NAME	INSTITUTION
Professor C R Emmanuel	University of Glasgow
Professor J R Edwards	University of Wales College of Cardiff
Professor N Garrod	University of Glasgow
Professor R H Gray	University of Dundee
Professor D Hatherly	University of Edinburgh
Professor D Heald	University of Aberdeen
Professor J Innes	University of Dundee
Professor I Lapsley	University of Edinburgh
Professor T Lee	University of Alabama
Professor R J Limmack	University of Stirling
Professor W M McInnes	University of Stirling
Professor K T Maunders	University of Hull
Professor F Mitchell	University of Edinburgh
Professor R H Parker	University of Exeter
Professor M J Sherer	University of Essex
Sir David Tweedie	Accounting Standards Board
Professor P Walton	Université de Genève
Professor G Whittington	University of Cambridge

The Research Committee is grateful to all those who participate in the refereeing process.

Inside Hospital Trusts:
Management Styles,
Accounting Constraints

by

Irvine Lapsley and Sue Llewellyn
with Gavin Burnett

The Institute of Public Sector Accounting Research (IPSAR)
at the University of Edinburgh

Published by
The Institute of Chartered Accountants of Scotland
27 Queen Street, Edinburgh EH2 1LA

First Published 1998
The Institute of Chartered Accountants of Scotland

© 1998
ISBN 1 871250 61 7

This book is published for the Research Committee of
The Institute of Chartered Accountants of Scotland.
The views expressed in this report are those of the authors
and do not necessarily represent the views of
the Council of the Institute or the Research Committee.

Printed by Bell and Bain Ltd, Glasgow

CONTENTS

Foreword..*i*
Acknowledgments...*iii*
Executive Summary...*v*

1 INTRODUCTION **1**
The antecedents of the internal market 5
The emergence of the hospital in the market 8
The market in operation 15
Research questions 17
Research method 18

2 HEALEY HOSPITAL **21**
Background 21
The executive team 21
Clinical directors 25
The non executive directors 28
Conclusion 31

3 MORGAN HOSPITAL **33**
Background 33
The executive team 33
Clinical directors 36
Non executive directors 40
Conclusion 42

4 TALBOT HOSPITAL **45**
Background 45
The executive team 45
Clinical directors 49
Non executive directors 55
Conclusion 57

5 CONCLUSION **59**
The impact of accounting on the management of trust hospitals 59
The operation of the market 60
Adequacy of the financial framework for hospital trusts 62
The effectiveness of clinical directorates 62
The role of non executive board members 63
Hospital management 64
The future of hospital trusts 65

REFERENCES **67**

APPENDIX A THEMATIC INTERVIEWS **71**
Executive team 71
Clinical directors 72
Non executive directors 73

TABLES

Page

Table 1.1   *Selected media comments on hospital trusts*.......................*3*

Table 1.2   *Statutory framework for self governing hospital trusts*............*10*

Table 1.3   *Devolution of management responsibility to self governing hospital trusts: major powers and entitlements*...................*13*

Table 1.4   *The financial regime of hospital trusts*...........................*14*

FOREWORD

The creation of self governing hospital trusts, as part of the 1989 NHS reforms, was one of the most radical government initiatives to improve hospital management. The concept of the hospital trust was based on the devolution of management powers to encourage local decision making aimed at creating a more responsive service.

The focus of this study is the effect of management in self governing hospital trusts. This is done by examining the experiences of three such trusts. Whilst the findings support the policy change signalled by the 1997 White Paper on the future of the NHS in Scotland, the study also identifies major issues for the efficient and effective organisation and delivery of health care which need to be addressed. These, this year, include the perceived defects in the market mechanisms as well as the difficulties faced by hospital management teams comprising clinicians, senior executives and non executive board members.

The Research Committee of The Institute of Chartered Accountants of Scotland considers that this publication is a timely and useful contribution to the current discussions concerning the reorganisation of the NHS.

John Baillie
Convener, Research Committee

May 1998

ACKNOWLEDGMENTS

We wish to express our gratitude to those members of staff in the hospital trusts included in this study who gave up their time for interviews and discussions, despite their extensive commitments. The research team would also like to record its gratitude to Colin McDaid who acted as research assistant on the project in the preliminary stages.

In conducting this research, the interpretation and analysis of the problems of hospital management have benefited from a number of sources. The Research Committee of The Institute of Chartered Accountants of Scotland had sight of the initial proposal and interim findings and the project has benefited from the constructive comments of its members. Irvine Lapsley has also presented papers on the themes discussed within this report and the comments obtained have been most useful in framing this report. In August 1996, he presented a paper on management styles in hospital management at the annual conference of the International Association of Management in Toronto. Useful comments on this work were obtained from participants at that conference and in particular, from Regina Herzlinger (Harvard) and Dana Forgione (Baltimore).

Irvine Lapsley has also presented a series of seminars on issues of clinical budgeting at the Judge Institute of Management Studies, Cambridge University; at the Department of Management Studies, St Andrews University; and at Warwick University Business School. Useful comments were received on this issue from participants at these seminars, but particularly from Sandra Dawson, Richard Barker and Geoffrey Whittington (Cambridge); Mo Malek (St Andrews); and Stan Brignall and Brendan McSweeney (Warwick). Irvine Lapsley has also presented on the broader issue of the hospital in the market at the University of Ca Foscari, Venice and the Technische Universität Muenchen. Helpful comments were received from participants at these seminars, but particularly from Giuseppe Marcon and Fabrizio Panozzo (Venice) and from Dieter Witt and Hilmar Sturm (Muenchen).

We would also like to thank Professor Pauline Weetman, Director of Research and Ann Lamb, Assistant Director at The Institute of Chartered Accountants of Scotland for their assistance throughout this project. Thanks also to Isobel Webber, Personal Secretary to the Director of Research for her care in typesetting this report.

Finally we would like to thank The Institute of Chartered Accountants of Scotland and the Research Committee for their financial support for this project which is one of a series being undertaken by the Institute of Public Sector Accounting Research (IPSAR) at the University of Edinburgh.

Irvine Lapsley

Sue Llewellyn

Gavin Burnett

Executive Summary

Hospital trusts have been a constant source of media attention. These are important organisations with a fundamental influence on the lives of the communities which they serve. There have been various government initiatives to improve hospital management. This particular study has examined the management of three hospitals in three different health boards in Scotland. The focus of this study was on the effect of management in the new environment: the hospital in the market. The study was undertaken by interviewing three tiers of management: executive team (full time, senior management); clinical directors (hospital doctors, with budgetary responsibility for clinical activity); and non executive directors, members of the trust hospitals' boards of directors.

Key issues arising from the case studies include:

- the impact of accounting on the management of these hospitals;
- the effectiveness of the operation of the internal market;
- the adequacy of the overall financial regulation of these hospitals;
- the problems of managing these hospitals, in particular the effectiveness of clinical directorates (budgets for clinical activity, with a designated budget holder) and of non executive directors of Trust boards; and
- the future of hospital trusts.

The impact of accounting

This study reveals a definite impact of accounting on the daily life of these hospitals, but in an unexpected way. All the formal systems of budgeting control are in place, with the normal cycle of planning and reporting actual results, on a monthly basis, to budget holders. While these formal systems are an important part of the financial control systems of these hospitals, the dominant way in which accounting impacts on the organisation is in the annual search for efficiency savings. These efficiency savings are set as part of the funding of these hospitals, with a 3% reduction in the budgets in 1996-97. This process, however, has been in place for a decade. The cumulative effect of the annual search for such savings in a labour intensive service is rationalisation, re-organisation and a reduction of services. All the hospital managements included in this study reported on this as a most significant challenge.

The effectiveness of the operation of the internal market

While the search for efficiency savings is a dominant feature of the management of these hospital trusts, this contrasts with the setting in which these hospitals operate. The creation of the internal market in health care in 1991 was intended to foster competition in the provision of health care. This, however, has not operated as intended. While there is competition between provider units, at the margin, the general tendency in these case studies is for the local health boards (which have responsibility for health care within specific geographical areas) to act as a monopoly purchaser of services from its main provider unit which is, in effect, a monopoly supplier. This is an outcome of the incapability of health care operating as a market where there are significant local monopolies which are the result of past decisions to locate hospitals in areas of dispersed population. Indeed, the only inkling of competition is within urban centres, where there are multiple hospital provider units. This situation is exacerbated by the defects of the key mechanism by which the market was intended to operate, namely the contracts set between purchasers (health boards and, in some cases, GP fundholders) and the providers (the hospital trusts). The contract setting arrangements have become an annual round of intense conflict as purchasers with reducing budgets for purchasing health care seek to ensure the attainment of similar, or better, levels of service as in previous years are obtained from providers, the hospital trusts, who receive fewer resources to meet these demands. This has, understandably, created tensions between the two contracting parties. More fundamentally, the settings in which these contracts were agreed were too short run, with a focus on an annual cycle of contracts. In a service with high fixed costs and increasing demands, this annual cycle works against long term planning. A major consequence of this is pragmatism and short termism, as hospital managers search for efficiency savings, more appropriately described as cost savings.

The adequacy of overall financial regulation

The third major result concerns the system of financial regulation of trust hospitals. This system will be familiar to those interested in the regulation of public corporations: the requirement to break even on revenue account, the target return on capital employed of 6% and the external financing limit which is a constraint on borrowing by these hospitals. This is the standard set of requirements for the financial regulation of public corporations. In these case studies, this system of regulation was somewhat remote from the management of these hospitals. The system was over specified, with no need for two profit targets. More importantly, the idea of a target return on capital employed, of such precision, and uniformity, devalued the merits of having a profit target. This was seen, and became, more of a technical accounting exercise than a fundamental tool of management. Furthermore, the external financing limit was not seen as a constraint, but as a source of frustration by the management of these hospital trusts and a denial of their expected 'freedoms', including the opportunity to borrow.

The problems of hospital management

The foregoing accentuate the difficulties of managing these hospitals. In this sense, the world of the hospital is a bracing, challenging environment for managers. In this study, the perceptions of key members of hospital management teams underline this. There are three dimensions which were addressed in this study, specifically the views of:

- clinical directors, *ie* hospital doctors who hold budgets for clinical activities;
- the hospital's core senior management, *ie* the executive team; and
- the non executive directors introduced into health boards.

From the clinical directors there is a long history of attempts to introduce effective clinical budgeting systems in hospitals. This is not a statement of failure, but one of complexity. There are major issues (of the nature of information technology support, management structures, the relevance of conventional financial information to the decision making of clinicians) which have prevented these systems taking hold effectively in hospitals. All of the hospitals in this study had installed these systems, but the devolved budgets were still in their infancy.

The senior management, the executive teams, found the management of these hospitals constrained by the defects of the market, the problems of the annual contracting cycle and the adversarial positions adopted in securing resources for their hospitals. Within these trusts, however, the researchers observed what they described as a 'new management dynamic' *ie* the management of these hospitals were prepared to take difficult decisions, and they acted more promptly than their predecessors in the old directly managed units, where management was often characterised by delays and the avoiding of difficult decisions. This was an undoubted benefit of the new hospital trust set up, but this is a benefit which was softened by the constraints on management, as described above.

The third component of management was that of the non executive directors of boards. These members of boards were lay members appointed by the Secretary of State for their expertise. The intention behind these appointments was to add breadth to the accumulated expertise of hospital management. In particular, but not solely, members with a business background who had a sound knowledge of business principles (management by results, the need for strategy, the management of change) were appointed to bring this 'business awareness' to bear in the conduct of the hospitals' management. The findings of this study, however, suggest that this is a role which has experienced limited success. The non executive directors, in general, expressed feelings of frustration and an inability to influence events. In part, this was a question of other pressures on their time. A major exception to this, however, in the three case studies, was the role of the chairman. In these studies, the chairman had significant business expertise and had been involved, in a significant way, in setting strategy for their hospital trusts. This raised issues about the governance and accountability of these non executive directors.

The future of hospital trusts

Overall, this study has reaffirmed the merits of the 'trust' concept. The devolved management of these hospitals has, by and large, worked well, on the basis of our findings. There are difficulties, however, for example: the future of non executive directors needs re-evaluation; also the devolution of budgets to clinical directors needs to be monitored. Nevertheless, the significant issues covered in this study are the extent to which the management of these hospitals were constrained by the non operation of the market, and by the short termism of the annual contracting cycle. Also, the financial framework for the regulation of these hospitals is over specified and remote from management, not only because of its precise requirements, but also because of the circumstances of hospital management in trusts, the search for efficiency savings, the 'operation' of the market in an intended way and the short termism of contracting.

The hospital trusts have a future as responsive organisations. The environment in which they operate, however, is a major constraint on them fulfilling their potential. The continuation of the trust concept (Scottish Office, 1997) does not, in itself, ameliorate these problems. In particular, there are major issues over:

* planning and coordination in the absence of the purchaser/provider split;
* the demise of small, responsive hospital trusts by large scale bureaucracies;
* the need for more refined financial instruments than cash releasing efficiency savings (CRES); and
* the opportunity for trusts to work within their original stated freedoms.

CHAPTER 1

INTRODUCTION

The emergence of hospital trusts as part of the internal market reforms of the National Health Service (NHS) introduced by the government of the day in the 1989 White Paper *Working for Patients* (Department of Health, 1989a) and enacted under the National Health Service and Community Care Act 1990, has aroused considerable controversy. The extent of the radical nature of this change can be gleaned from figure 1, which depicts the situation in simple terms, before and after the introduction of the internal market changes on 1 April 1991.

Figure 1 The Organisation of the NHS in Scotland: Pre- and Post the 1991 Reforms

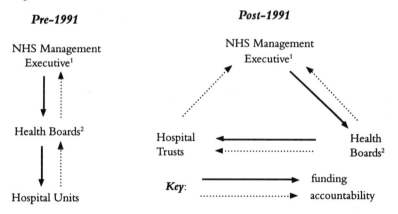

Pre-1991

NHS Management Executive[1]

Health Boards[2]

Hospital Units

Post-1991

NHS Management Executive[1]

Hospital Trusts

Health Boards[2]

Key:

→ funding

┈┈┈▶ accountability

Notes:

[1] That part of the executive, the Scottish Office, which allocates funds and oversees the Scottish Health Service.

[2] Medical and lay members, appointed by the Secretary of State, with responsibility for health care provision in specific geographical areas. The English equivalent is health authorities.

This figure shows that the old style vertical accountability was swept away and replaced by a set of relationships in which the new style hospital trusts were in a position to negotiate with their local and other health boards and GP fundholders, where these existed. This contrasts, markedly, from the previous relationships where funds were allocated by health boards directly to hospital units which were managed directly by the health boards. However, a critical element of the internal market was the potential for competition. Appleby *et al* (1990) expressed concern about the likelihood of local hospitals being local monopoly suppliers of health care, undermining the concept of a competitive market. As this study shows, this problem, the existence of local monopsonies, was also a concern in the Scottish health care system.

In this study, the everyday life of hospital trusts is examined from a management perspective: the views of key actors, senior managers, non executives and clinical directors, in this new form of hospital organisation. The perspective adopted in this investigation is contextual. To understand the practices and processes in present day hospital management, we need to explore the antecedents of the initiatives which brought about current management structures and the environment in which they operate. While we focus here on specific initiatives which were directed at improving the efficiency of hospital operations, it is also important to recognise that, in the NHS, there have been frequent reorganisations and restructurings which have culminated in a turbulent environment. All of these changes have been cited as demotivating, or even demoralising NHS staff. An example of this is the citation of the following quotation by Caius Petronius, in a commentary on the NHS reforms by a leading expert on the NHS (Maynard, 1989, p.15):

> *We trained very hard, but it seemed that every time we were beginning to form up into teams, we would be reorganised. I was to learn later in life that we tend to meet any new situation by reorganising, and a wonderful method it can be for creating the illusion of progress, while producing confusion, inefficiency and demoralisation. [Caius Petronius, AD66]*

This picture, of confusion and tension, can also be gleaned from the media view of the activities of hospitals in the post reform era. Examples of the kinds of comments made in the media on hospital trusts are shown in table 1.1. This presents a fragmentary picture, one in which finance and accounting dominate and in which the provision of health care appears to be in jeopardy from this managerial orientation in the hospitals of the 1990s. In this study, we seek to examine these new management processes and practices in hospitals to determine whether these criticisms, of a supplanting of the caring professions by the managerial and financial, of a subverting of the aims of health care delivery by a slavish concern for financial results and efficiency gains, can be substantiated.

As part of this process, we not only present the findings of our investigation of the management of three NHS hospital trusts, but we also examine, objectively, the impact of important earlier initiatives and the merits of existing commentaries on the workings of the internal market in health care. Before a consideration of what hospital trusts are, or are intended to be, and their role in the new market, we examine the antecedents of the internal market.

Table 1.1: Selected media comments on hospital trusts

Hospital consultants have warned that acute bed closures will put an intolerable strain on health services in Scotland. Consultants from 5 hospitals in Glasgow have denounced as unfeasible plans by the Scottish Office to cut acute beds by one third by the year 2000. One stated: 'We do not have 30 people stacked up every night in casualty like they do in London, but the Scottish Office is determined to drive us down the English route. (Scottish NHS Faces Crisis Over Bed Cuts), *Public Finance*, 8 April 1994.

So far all the movement towards local pay has been for non clinical staff. South Tees says that (clinical staff) is its next step. That should be a battle worth seeing. It will take a brave Trust to take on the might of the professions. Steven Brown, *Public Finance*, 6 May 1994.

The head of the health service has ordered one of Scotland's biggest hospital trusts to hire experts to find a way out of a deepening crisis which threatens its financial viability. F Urquhart, *The Scotsman,* 27 September 1995.

Neither Grampian Health Board nor the Association of GP Fundholders in Grampian has signed funding contracts for this year with Aberdeen Royal Hospitals NHS Trust though the basis for agreement has been reached. Both contracts should have been rubber stamped six months ago but have been delayed because of the trust's funding problems. F Urquhart, *The Scotsman,* 29 September 1995.

As many as 14 Scottish health trusts could compete in an unprecedented takeover battle to run two hospitals in Fife. Health Trusts Battle Over Fife Hospitals, Sue Leonard, *The Scotsman,* 24 December, 1995.

A stark warning has been issued about an impending financial crisis at the main Borders hospital, which could lead to job losses for staff and longer waiting times for patients. Borders Hospital give warning of financial crisis, Bryan Christie, *The Scotsman,* 21 February 1996.

Patients' lives are being threatened by an NHS accounting system that punishes the most successful hospitals, according to senior consultants. They say that the situation is so serious that care is nearing meltdown. Flagship hospital trusts are reportedly seeing their once efficient departments slowly destroyed by government requirements for trusts to make year-on-year efficiency savings of 3 per cent. But they are not allowed to use any surpluses to increase capital resources, such as beds in the following financial year. Instead they have to use them to cut prices. Doctors Condemn NHS Trust Financing, *The Times,* 17 May 1996.

A senior clinician who was appointed medical director of the Borders General Hospital NHS trust last week has decided not to take up the post. Top Hospital Post Declined, *The Scotsman,* 23 July 1996.

Fears are rising that one of two £100m hospital building projects, flagships of the government's drive to attract private finance in to build Scotland's public services, may now be scrapped. PFI hospital project faces axe, Roland Main, *Scotland on Sunday,* 22 December, 1996.

The antecedents of the internal market

There are two distinct strands to the antecedents of 'the hospital in the market', *ie* hospital trusts in the internal market for health care, *viz:*

• management change; and
• accounting change

Here we discuss both prior to a discussion of hospital trusts and their place in the internal market. Both of these changes have been described by Lapsley (1994, 1997) as 'false revolutions', in the sense that neither of these changes achieved what they set out to do. Nevertheless, these changes can be seen as important precursors of the move to the *quasi* market, the foundations which made possible the creation of the hospital trust as a 'provider' in the market place.

Management change

The NHS was established in 1948 as a bureaucratic organisation in which professional groups, particularly medical professionals, played a dominant role. In the 1974 reorganisation of the NHS this multi professional bureaucracy was formalised in a system of consensus management in which there were tiers of management, at the level of regional, area, and district health authorities, and at which the professions had a significant, equal voice. In the famous review of this management system in 1983 by Sir Roy Griffiths (Griffiths, 1983) a number of serious criticisms, however, were levelled against consensus management. These included the following:

• institutionalised stagnation, *ie* resistance to change;
• excessive delays in decision making by management;
• avoidance of the resolution of contentious issues; and
• the domination of management by the medical profession.

In the face of these circumstances, Griffiths advocated a system of general management for each level of the service. In this recommendation, the reference point was comparability with the private sector. In the new management system there was to be a single person who was in charge and to whom other professionals would be accountable.

Griffiths envisaged that this new management system would lead to significant change in the operation of the NHS. These general managers were seen as 'change agents', key persons who would drive the NHS forward, seek out waste and inefficiencies and provide a stimulus for managerially driven improvements in the organisation and delivery of health care. The reality, however, proved to be very different. There was an expectation that these new style general managers would be drawn from outside the NHS, but, with a few exceptions, who typically did not stay in the NHS for long, these appointments were drawn from the administrative cadre of the NHS. As a result, the impact of general management was somewhat less than intended. There is evidence from numerous studies which indicate that general management behaviour was risk averse; was based on coalitions of power rather than the imposition of a single authority figure; and that management exhibited caution in challenging the medical profession. Further details of such studies are available in Lapsley (1993, 1994, 1997). This picture, of limited impact, is linked closely to the second change mentioned above *ie* accounting change in the NHS.

Accounting change

The accounting change we refer to here is not changes in financial accounting practice, but in management accounting, particularly in the area of devolved budgets. However, while this is the most evident formal change in accounting which was likely to be of major importance in impacting on behaviour, we were sensitive to the emergence of other mechanisms by which decisions on the allocation of resources and their control are made. In this respect the issue of targets imposed on hospital trusts as cash releasing efficiency savings, which resulted in reductions in funding, in real terms, to those trusts was a matter of considerable significance as explored further in this report.

As mentioned above the advocacy of devolved budgets is linked to the failure of general management to make its intended impact, as one of the key levers by which changes could be wrought in the organisation and delivery of health care services. Historically, health care management has had a major focus on staying within cash limited expenditure. This focus, with limited devolved budgets, mainly to ancillary and support services, left clinicians at several removes from budgetary processes. The outcome was geared to the achievement of financial equilibrium, but not necessarily to effective use of the resources at the disposal of the hospital.

It was in the above context that, in the wake of the limited impact of the general management initiative, there were successive initiatives to devolve budgets further in hospitals and bring the medical profession into this sphere of budgetary responsibility. The first of these initiatives, management budgeting, is an outcome of the Griffiths report. A progress report in 1985 (DHSS, 1985) noted considerable difficulties and the need for a change of direction. Subsequently, this particular initiative was re-labelled 'resource management' (DHSS, 1986). This was an attempt to shift the focus of budgets for clinicians away from the purely financial to encompass both financial and non financial information. This latter type of information was to include activity statistics and medical information on treatment patterns, patient characteristics and outcomes.

These particular initiatives are widely regarded as failures. Indeed, the formal evaluation of the latter of the above initiatives for the Department of Health by Packwood et al (1991) concluded that progress on resource management had been slow and patchy and that they had observed implementation, rather than implementation and practice. Perrin (1988) documented the obstacles to making such systems operational (op cit p.105):

> ...There are behavioural problems for clinicians in accepting accountability and discipline for the costs of the resources they cause to be consumed in aiding patients. There are behavioural problems for the nursing and paramedical professions in accepting that ... consultant doctors are the natural managers of the total hospital services. There are financial problems in terms of the limited resources available for the rapid upgrading and computerisation of activity or workload information systems capable

of supporting an accurate clinical budgeting system with prompt reporting of performance/variances at monthly intervals. There are staffing problems as regards providing sufficient skilled unit financial advisers (or management accountants), given current NHS salary scales and constraints on management costs and grading structures.

Despite this catalogue of obstacles and difficulties, however, Perrin remained optimistic that these were not insuperable and that, ultimately, operational systems would be feasible. It is instructive to note that the above verdicts of 'failure to date', coincide with the creation of the internal market. This raises the possibility that these changes, both in management and accounting, would fare better in the new market oriented environment. This possibility is an important strand in this investigation. To explore further how such a possibility might be realised we turn next to the 'hospital in the market' to examine more closely the likelihood of such failures becoming success stories.

The emergence of the hospital in the market

The above initiatives had been tried, with limited success, to change the shape and direction of the NHS. These can be seen as antecedents of the market, in the sense that these failures prompted a review of the NHS which led to the creation of the internal or *quasi* market.

The NHS market was described as 'internal' or a '*quasi* market', because the purchasers of health care, GP fundholders and Health Boards/Authorities, were funded by general taxation and the patient, 'the consumer', did not purchase health care directly from providers, such as hospital trusts. This concept is generally attributed to Enthoven (1985). The fundamental aim of this internal market in health care was to increase the efficiency of health care delivery by promoting competition for patients. The means by which this was to be achieved was a redesignation of the responsibilities of health authorities and hospitals (previously locked together in a vertically integrated relationship) such that there is a purchaser (health authority)/provider (hospital trust) split, with the purchaser placing contracts with the provider organisations. In addition, there were other purchasers in the shape of GP fundholders (see Lapsley *et al*, 1997). There were three forms for such contracts (DOH, 1989a):

* block - a single lump sum payment for a range of services;
* cost and volume - in which the contractual payment is varied for additions in activity beyond the contract specification; and
* cost per case - in which contracts are set on the basis of agreed services at an agreed cost, per individual patient.

It was expected that, initially, contracts would be on a 'block' basis, with a progression towards 'cost per case'.

Contracting implies provider status and our particular focus is on the hospital trust, as a provider in the *quasi* market. The nature, and organisation, of the hospital trust as a provider in the *quasi* market is shown in table 1.2. This is the statutory framework for hospital trusts. It is evident from this table that, while these trusts are formally and accurately described as public corporations, they nevertheless owe a lot to private sector influences.

As table 1.2 sets out, there is a board of directors for each trust. This comprises both executive, full time appointments within the hospital trusts, and non executive members. The precise number of such posts is prescribed for the trust. In the case of the non executive directors, the Scottish Office (undated), has issued the following guidance as to who would be an appropriate appointee to the board of an NHS trust.

Table 1.2: Statutory framework for self governing hospital trusts

1. Each Trust is a body corporate having a board of directors consisting of a chairman, up to five executive directors and up to five non executive directors.

2. All directors are full and equal members of the board, with responsibility for:
    (i) determining the overall policies of the trust,
    (ii) monitoring the execution of the agreed policies,
    (iii) maintaining the financial viability of the trust.

3. Each Trust owns its assets, the land, hospital buildings and equipment necessary to fulfil its functions.

4. The value of these assets is matched by an originating capital debt, comprising:
    (i) interest bearing debt, with defined interest and repayment terms, and
    (ii) public dividend capital, with no fixed repayment on which the Trust pays dividends.

    This original capital debt is owed to the Exchequer. It is normally in the ratio of 50/50, for debt/public dividend capital.

Source: The NHS and Community Care Act, 1990, Section 5.

There are no prescribed qualifications but candidates are expected to have a general understanding of management; or relevant experience in the public or private sector. In addition active involvement in the local community would be particularly valuable.

In addition to the board structure owing much to private sector influences, so does the capital structure prescribed for hospital trusts. This has debt and public dividend capital, the public sector equivalent of equity capital, in a capital gearing ratio of 50/50.

On the composition of trust boards, Ashburner (1993) reported on a survey of English trusts which demonstrated that some two thirds of non executives had business experience. This early survey was confirmed by Ferlie *et al* (1996), which also reported that two-thirds of non executive directors, in both trusts and health authorities in this study, were employed in the private sector. This matter is addressed within this study. However, of more importance than the composition of the boards is the impact of such boards. This is a matter of concern in this investigation.

There is some prior research on this issue. After an investigation of the practices and conduct of one NHS trust board over an 18 month period, Peck (1993, p.84) concluded that:

> *The conclusion of the research on this board is that during the initial 18 months it failed to make a significant impact on the governance of the organisation. The presence of the observation data makes this a conclusion in which we can have confidence. This failure does not, in the light of previous research based on actors' accounts and minutes, constitute a major criticism of the individual board. Rather it suggests that trust boards will experience the same problems as other corporate boards in attempting to have an effective impact on the organisations over which they preside.*

Ashburner (1993), however, challenged the concept of measuring the effectiveness of trust boards, in the absence of any detailed guidance as to their intended role. The role in table 1.2 could be seen as vague and ambiguous. However, Ferlie *et al* (1996) took the perspective that there are two contrasting views over the functioning of trust boards. First, there was a view (Peck, 1995) which suggested that changes at the strategic apex of organisations does not and cannot effect the behaviour of key actors in the organisation at the operational level. This view suggested that this kind of reorganisation was no more than a 'superficial relabelling exercise' (*op.cit.* p.15). A second, contrasting view detected by Ferlie *et al* (*op.cit.*) was that these new boards presented the possibility of achieving substantive change. This view saw their new powers as substantially different from the previous era of health authority membership (widely criticised as 'rubber stamps', see Day and Klein, 1987; Best and Ham, 1989) and thus provided the opportunity for them to reshape the organisation of hospitals, from the top downwards.

The analysis by Ferlie *et al* (1996) was based on a typology of four levels at which non executive members of trust boards could impact on decisions:

Level A: a continuation of the historical situation, 'a rubber stamp';

Level B: the non executives probe and question proposals, and even send them back to the Executive for further consideration;

Level C: substantial involvement in deciding between strategic options and at an early stage in the process; and

Level D: the board debates and delineates a vision or strategic priorities for a future period in time.

This typology has been used by Ferlie *et al* as a frame of reference in assessing the impact of boards at case study sites in England. These sites included both trusts and health authorities. Of these study settings reported on by Ferlie *et al* (*op.cit.*), there were no sites at Level A, with the majority at Level B. Movement to Level C was most noticeable within NHS trusts rather than the health authorities. These findings and this framework informed our analysis of the impact of the non executives in the hospital trusts included in this study.

The concept of the hospital trust was based on devolution of management powers to encourage local decision making. This was with the intent of creating a more responsive service instead of the highly bureaucratic form of organisation which had existed previously. The freedoms which the trust management was to receive are shown in table 1.3.

Table 1.3: Devolution of management responsibility to self governing hospital trusts: major powers and entitlements

1. The power to acquire, own and dispose of assets to ensure the most effective use of them.
2. The power to borrow, subject to an annual financing limit.
3. Freedom to retain operating surpluses and build up reserves.
4. Freedom to set their own management structures without control from districts, regions or the NHS Management Executive.
5. Freedom to employ whatever, and however many, staff they consider necessary.
6. Freedom to determine pay and conditions of service for staff, and to conduct their own industrial relations.
7. Freedom to employ and direct their own medical and nursing staff.

Source: Department of Health, Working for Patients, Working Paper 1, Self Governing Hospitals, 1989b.

This is based on one of the initial working papers promulgated by the Department of Health in support of its White Paper, Working for Patients (DOH, 1989b). Within this scheme, there are three main strands:

• discretion over staffing (numbers, pay, conditions), for all categories of staff, see items 5 and 7;
• discretion over internal management free from intervention from other parts of the NHS (but see the tension with table 1.2, which prescribes a particular format for boards of hospital trusts); and
• financial freedoms, over acquisition of assets, financing and ability to make profits, see items 1, 2 and 3.

Table 1.4: The financial regime of hospital trusts

The financial obligations of hospital trusts, as specified in section 10 of the NHS and Community Care Act of 1990 are as follows:

1. Every NHS trust shall ensure that its revenue is not less than sufficient, taking one financial year with another, to meet outgoings properly chargeable to the revenue account.

2. It shall be the duty of every NHS trust to achieve such financial objectives as may from time to time be set by the Secretary of State with the Consent of the Treasury and as are applicable to it; and any such objectives may be made applicable to NHS trusts generally, or to a particular NHS trust or to NHS trusts of a particular description.

3. Under (2) above, NHS trusts are required to both:
   (i) meet their external financing limit (EFL)
   (ii) achieve a 6% return on the average value of net assets

As part of this investigation we examine the extent to which such freedoms were realised by hospital trusts in the internal market. In this regard, it is important to note that the initial position on financial freedoms (as presented in table 1.3) has been modified twice. These modifications are shown in table 1.4.

The first modification came with the passing of the NHS and Community Care Act of 1990. This clarified the fundamental financial obligation of trusts as 'breaking even, taking one year with another' (see (1), table 1.4). This is the familiar financial obligation given to public corporations which was first introduced with the initial nationalisations of utilities in the 1940s and 1950s. The second modification is that of the right of the Secretary of State to set specific financial targets. This is a shift from the initial injunction or freedom to earn surpluses to more specific guidance *ie* the 6% return on capital employed. Closer examination of the method of accounting for capital shows, however, that in practice, profits of NHS trusts may be greater, in private sector terms. While the new method of capital accounting introduced to the NHS as part of these reforms is described as being comparable to the private sector, it is not (see DOH, 1989; Lapsley, 1990). Basically, private sector companies compute the depreciation charge as a deduction from income on the basis of the historical cost of assets held. In the NHS, the depreciation charge is based on the current replacement cost of assets held plus a notional charge as a proxy for the financing of assets held. If the profits of a trust were converted to the private sector basis, an apparently more attractive profitable performance may be evident.

This financial framework has already been the subject of review in England (NHS Executive, 1996). This review concluded that (*op.cit.* para 6)

... *the regime is fundamentally sound. Nevertheless, some aspects would benefit from clarification and others had the potential to create perverse incentives or distortions within the market.*

This issue, the operation of the financial framework, is investigated in this study, in respect of its impact on the management of the specific trusts included in this study.

The market in operation

The previous section described the framework within which hospital trusts are expected to operate. Before proceeding to an examination of the specific research questions posed in this project and the consideration of the evidence gathered, we examine briefly available evidence on the operation of the internal market in the NHS.

As yet, there is limited information on the behaviour of trusts, with most research to date focusing on GP fundholders and their role in the internal market. However, at the time of the announcement of these market reforms for health care, there was concern expressed over the likely outcomes of the market initiative. One issue was the ability of provider units to compete (Lapsley, 1993). This may be limited because of the specialised nature of some facilities (*eg* heart surgery). Also, as Appleby *et al* (1990) noted, there was the circumstance of spatial monopoly in which there may be only one provider unit with a local monopoly. A further predicted consequence of the implementation of the internal market was the result of 'winners' and 'losers' within provider units (Lapsley, 1993). In this scenario, the successful hospitals have the potential to attract more patients and resources. Large modern hospitals, with economies of scale and lower unit costs, therefore have the prospect of gaining most from the market, and relatively costly hospitals, with a lack of modern facilities, have the prospect of losing out (Mohan, 1990).

The above concerns of how the market would operate have been accentuated by the nature of contract setting and the possibilities for these trusts to undertake opportunistic behaviour. As part of this evolution of the market, the role of accounting is of considerable importance. At the time of the reforms, one of the leading hospital trusts in England, expressed concern about its ability to generate accurate internal costing information for contract setting (Laurence, 1991a and 1991b). This state of affairs has been confirmed by subsequent research (King et al, 1994a, 1994b). As trusts seek to enhance their accounting capability in the market place, there may be concomitant effects on the dominance of the medical profession in hospitals (Lapsley, 1993). This raises important questions about the integration of hospital consultants into the management of hospitals, which are addressed in this study.

One study of hospital trusts in England (Propper and Bartlett, 1997), reported that market forces had 'real, though variable' (op.cit. p.28) effects on health care provision. That study suggests that despite local monopoly power, there is a tendency for the catchment areas of hospitals to overlap, thereby creating a potential for competition, which is further supported by the inability of all hospitals to compete on equal terms, on all specialities. One key finding stressed by Propper and Bartlett (op.cit.) was the reactive stance of many trusts to the opportunities created by the existence of fundholding GPs seeking favourable contracts. However, there was limited information from this study on the behaviour of trusts on pricing. It appears that, for fundholding GPs, there were other considerations which dominated in contracting (eg quality of service considerations). See Lapsley, Llewellyn and Grant (1997) for further evidence of this behaviour by these GPs.

To date, the actions and behaviour of trusts and trust management in the market remain areas about which little is known. This study aims to contribute to the debate on the future of trusts by addressing these issues.

Research questions

In studying the above issues in the context of hospital trusts we adopted a two tier approach to this investigation. At one level, the overarching perspective, we pursued two particular themes:

• What is the role of accounting information in the management of the trust? Is it supportive, enhancing issues, constraining, ignored?
• Are financial targets and controls (the External Financing Limit, the target return on capital employed, balancing the revenue account) too constraining on the activities of trusts?

These themes constitute a framework or background against which the second tier, more focused, research questions explore management practices in the hospital trusts included in this study:

1. Has the management of hospital trusts provided a new dynamic in appraising their trusts opportunities and (re)shaping its priorities?
2. Has the devolving of financial responsibilities to trusts resolved the long standing difficulties of involving hospital doctors in financial management?
3. Have non executive board members brought a new business awareness to the activities of hospitals?

Question 1 addresses the issue of the extent to which the management practices of hospitals, long characterised as exhibiting reluctance to change and act, have captured the 'dynamic' of addressing and initiating changes in the provision of services. Questions 2 and 3 address the mechanisms by which this 'dynamic' is brought into operation: the devolution of budgets to clinical directors; and the presence of non executives were to be appointed on the grounds that their business experience or 'awareness' could prove invaluable in the effective operation of trusts.

Research questions 1 to 3 are examined in the case studies of the hospitals included in this study, with reference made to the overarching questions throughout the discussion of these cases. Before considering the detailed case study results, we describe our research method.

Research method

This study seeks to investigate the everyday reality (Tomkins and Groves, 1983) of the management of hospital trusts. The focus of this study is on key actors or influential persons (Pettigrew, 1992), who take part in the management of these trusts, to elicit their views on the process of management. This perspective recognises the potential for a significant agency impact (Giddens, 1984) in the shaping and implementation of this particular NHS reform.

The basic focus of this research is on case study settings. This is now well recognised as a method of investigation which facilitates the study of phenomena in more depth and which is amenable to the study of accounting in organisations (Kaplan, 1986). The three case study settings in this study are all general hospitals each of which is in a different health board area. Two of them, named Healey and Morgan for reasons of confidentiality, are district general hospitals. The third, named Talbot for reasons of confidentiality, is a major teaching hospital. These study settings embrace a city centre location, a rural location and an industrial location. This provides a cross section of hospitals to present a more representative picture of the experiences of managers in the Scottish health service.

There is the caveat that managers' perceptions of the effectiveness of their actions are subjective and may distort actual effectiveness. Within these case study settings, however, we seek to achieve a triangulation (Denzin, 1978) by exploring the views of these separate constituencies in the management network of hospital trusts, viz the executive team, the non executive members of the trust board and clinical directors.

Thematic interviews were conducted with each of these groups by a member of the research team. The interview checklists are contained at Appendix A. Each of these interviews lasted approximately one hour, with some lasting considerably longer. The results of these interviews are presented as three case studies of each these study settings. The research findings from these studies, particularly in the case of the clinical directors, are presented as a narrative (Sayer, 1992) which describes, analyses and interprets the experiences of managing the hospital trust. In addition to these interviews, the research team also gathered factual data, reports, financial information and other accounts of the experiences of these hospital trusts. From all of this, the aim is to present an overview of management's perceptions, and the role of accounting, in the management of hospital trusts.

CHAPTER 2

HEALEY HOSPITAL

Background

Healey hospital employs around 1,700 clinical and support staff of which some 51% are in the medical and nursing areas. It has a total of 490 beds. In a typical year, this Trust treats some 30,000 in-patients and day patients, and almost 130,000 out-patients. The local health board is the main purchaser of Healey's services and there are few GP fundholders in this area. In contracting with its local health board, Healey is set targets for the waiting time before it sees its patients. Healey met all its targets for in-patients and day case treatment for specialities, except one, at which 94% of patients were seen within the prescribed target. We examine the perceptions of the three elements of this Trust's management, as follows: the executive team; the clinical directors; and non executive directors.

The executive team

At Healey hospital, the executive team comprises: the chief executive, who has considerable experience of NHS management and started his career in nursing; a medical director who previously worked as a surgeon, at this hospital; a director of nursing and quality, who was recruited from another NHS hospital; a director of human resources, who has considerable experience of the personnel function within the NHS, but started as a nurse; and a director of finance who has extensive, senior experience within the finance function in both the private and public sectors.

The management team at Healey hospital does function as a team. The chief executive may exercise his authority, if necessary, but in general the team meets regularly to discuss the substantive business of the trust. There are formal agendas, discussions of policy and operational issues, decisions on the way forward and agreed action, with full minutes of the meetings. Members of the team have an input to the formulation of agendas. There are routine matters, such as budget reports, contract reports, quality monitoring, the capital programme review, and clinical audit policies, but other matters, such as emergency admissions, contingency plans may be included in agendas. In addition, the trust board oversees and monitors the implementation of these objectives, its major focus being strategic. The management operates within the context of an explicit business strategy, with a hierarchy of objectives, strategic and operational, which provide the starting point for the formal objectives of individual members of the management team. This executive seeks to be proactive and has created a number of initiatives, particularly on 'quality' issues but also on issues of the organisation of professional care, with links with a commercial, education company. On the finance side it has undertaken a private finance initiative (PFI) project to purchase a body scanner.

Constraints facing management team

This management team is striving to bring a new dynamic to the operation of this hospital, but it faces a number of inhibiting constraints. The major constraint is the acute hospital services review being undertaken by the local health board. However, there are also significant challenges which this hospital management faces on the operational side in terms of setting contracts in the internal market and achieving cash releasing efficiency savings.

Acute hospital services review

The acute hospital services review is a study of the major issues facing the local health board, as purchaser, and of the delivery of health care in future years. At present, Healey hospital offers a full range of hospital services as a general hospital. There is also a neighbouring general hospital offering similar facilities. The review was established to examine a range of possibilities including the potential for centralisation of acute services, with the closure of one of these hospitals or the creation of complementary sites, with one focusing on acute and the other hospital concentrating on more specialist services. This review has created major uncertainties for the management of Healey hospital. One source of frustration is that one of the reasons advanced for the need for an acute hospital services review is the recruitment and retention of medical staff. Healey, however, maintains that is has no difficulty in recruiting medical staff either at consultant level or more junior staff. A negative side effect of the review is the length of time which it has taken to make the announcement, against a background of considerable speculation that it was going to happen, and the length of time before the review is completed. A consequence of this has been the delay of long term plans because of the uncertainties of the outcome of the review. Specifically, at Healey, plans to upgrade medical wards in some of the older buildings on this site have been delayed because it was considered that, given the uncertainties of the acute services review, it would not be possible to attract PFI monies. Healey hospital management, however, have pressed ahead with the purchase of a CT scanner and the opening of an additional operating theatre.

Setting contracts in the internal market

The Healey hospital management team have found the entire contracting process in the new internal market an extremely frustrating process. Healey hospital receives over 90% of its contractual income from its local health board. It also has contracts with three other health boards, with the three GP fundholders in the area and has extra contractual referrals. Nevertheless, the bulk of its income and the major focus of its negotiations is with the local health board. In these negotiations, members of Healey's hospital management decried their description as contracting. In their view, this was not contract negotiation, but a means of making funding allocations by the health board. Despite extensive discussions or 'negotiations' with the local health board, the amount of services purchased are more akin to the previous year's allocation with an adjustment, which may be positive or negative, for inflation and other, notably efficiency, effects. This entire process was described by the management of Healey as extremely time consuming. The hospital management at Healey had made considerable effort to involve senior clinicians in these exchanges with the local health board. As one senior executive stated, a consequence of this was that:

> *we now have a big concern that the clinicians are becoming disenchanted with the contracting process. They can't see the results obtained for the time which they have been involved in the negotiation ...*

Achieving cash releasing efficiency savings

The final major constraint on the actions of the Healey hospital management team was the drive for cash releasing efficiency savings. For the current year, the income which it received from the local health board had an uplift of 2.5% for inflation. From this amount there was then a 3.0% reduction made for efficiency gains. As the chief executive stated:

> *... this is our dilemma, we have standstill income with activity increasing and salary increases to be met ...*

In the current year, and the previous year, the hospital management had managed to survive, with difficulty. Part of this process had been the amelioration of the worst effects of the efficiency targets by the appropriation of resources to minimise service losses, but this option was not available to the trust in the following year. As one senior executive commented:

> *... there comes a point when you can't get efficiency savings, something's got to give and then it's a case of which service do you not want?*

Despite these constraints, the management of Healey welcomed the concept of the hospital as a trust. They spoke favourably of the greater freedom which they possessed to take decisions, locally, which gave them a greater sense of control. It also, in their view, speeded up management decision making.

Clinical directors

There are five clinical directorates at this hospital: medicine; surgery; gynaecology and paediatrics; clinical resources; and diagnostic and paramedical services, reflecting its status as a district general hospital. Clinical resources is headed up by a non medical director whose background is pharmacy, a very unusual event in directorate structures. The overall ethos of the directorates is very focused on personalities and there is a strongly held view that if the right individuals are in the key posts then positive developments are likely. This hospital is in a directly competitive position *vis-à-vis* a neighbouring trust hospital; the clinical directors, as are other members of the hospital management, are very aware of these circumstances. The following discussion locates the interface of management and clinicians' views on financial information, and the relationship with the health board, as being the key issues for the directors interviewed.

The interface of management and clinicians

There is a widely held view at this hospital that relationships with management, or rather as one clinician director stated, 'non medical management' are good. The involvement of the clinicians in establishing the management structure was thought to be crucial in setting up a positive dialogue.

We have a good dialogue with the non medical managers. We, the clinicians, were involved right from the start, I think it's often been different in other trusts. We set up the management structure which is a good one. Also there's been an interchange of ideas and receptivity on both sides from the beginning. We had a very open exchange which I don't think exists in all the trusts. (CD1)

Having the 'right' individuals on the teams was thought to be crucial.

Working together depends on personalities, the structure can provide support but that's not really important. We have a good relationship with management going back to the 70s. (CD4)

Cooperation with management sometimes exceeded that between the individual directorates.

The interface with management is good. I find that the medical staff here are, in general, more cooperative than other places I've been, they are quite a rational bunch in the main. If anything there's more jockeying for position between the clinical directors themselves, territorial disputes, rather than between the non medical and the medical management. (CD3)

Where criticisms were expressed they were around perceptions that sometimes the clinical directors were not party to all the information and, hence, to the ultimate decisions made. In consequence, perhaps, discussions were sometimes around relatively trivial issues.

Basically we are on fairly good speaking terms but I still have a feeling, maybe it's paranoia, that we are not necessarily given all the information to hand. (CD5)

I'm not entirely convinced that we talk about the things which need to be addressed, like how do we retain staff in this market environment, important issues. The level of discussion is not as focused as it might be, it's a little bit sterile. (CD2)

The role of financial information

As in the interface with management, which was seen to revolve around the personalities involved, the quality of financial information was perceived as being dependent upon the individuals who interpreted it for clinicians.

We've had three people seconded from finance, the first offered valuable constructive comments to facilitate things and he offered advice on creative accounting. The second just produced finance sheets and never came up with answers. The third person is excellent and very sensitive to the needs of the directorate. The usefulness of financial information is related to the capabilities of the management accountant who is seconded to us. Hence first year great, second year hopeless, third year excellent. (CD2)

It's dependent upon the capacity of whatever management accountant we get, if they are lacking in imagination then the usefulness is diminished. If they can discuss our requirements and give us information that we didn't know we could get then that's great. They need to grasp our problems and see the accounting equivalent. (CD5)

As in the other trusts, linking information on the effectiveness of clinical activities with costs was seen to be the crucial area which required development.

I might know that operation X takes a big chunk of my budget but I haven't got the information to tell me how effective it is. So I can't account for what I do. (CD4)

There was, however, a perception that working with costing information was important.

I think that there has been a sea change in clinician's attitudes, quite a material change from there being a small core of clinicians interested in budgeting and costs and so on to there being a much more general feeling that these things are important.

The relationship with the health board

As with the other trusts, the relationship with the health board was a difficult one. Again in this trust this was conceptualised by the clinical directors as being dependent upon the individuals involved. Consequently upon the recent departure of the chair of the local health board, there was some hope of an improved dialogue, as the following comments illustrate:

It was very poor, being confrontational rather than cooperative in nature. But it has improved in the last year, the change of chairman has meant that it's become less politicised, well less overtly politicised anyway. (CD4)

There has to be change and further evolution. Of course we had a problem with the previous health board chairman who was forced to resign because of bias. (CD2)

The trust is dependent upon the health board as the prime purchaser because there are only three GP fundholders in the area.

In real terms we have one purchaser and they give us a contract but it's very little different from our old budget. We've only three GP fundholders so they've not made a big impact ... (CD1)

We have only one prime purchaser and that creates difficulties. We developed a tariff based approach but it just got torn up. It's a case of there's what you got last year and this is what you get this year. I think our board are more resistant to change than other health boards, basically they just don't operate the health service changes. There's no real market pressure, the purchaser has excess power ... (CD5)

This situation, again as with the other trusts, generates an expectation, or perhaps a hope, that the role of the health board will diminish through the centralisation of planning and the devolution of purchasing to primary care, as the following comment indicates:

I hope, rather than anticipate, that the role of the health boards will diminish, they could be limited to helping a more central body define local need. Purchasing power should pass to primary care. (CD2)

The non executive directors

The non executive directors at Healey hospital form a cohesive, well knit group. There are occasional differences, for example, the ideological divide over the appropriateness of having private medicine at this hospital. However, this group of non executives is a group of local persons, all of whom are committed to Healey hospital. Indeed, these non executives reported that they regularly attended more days than their contractual requirements at Healey.

The chairman at Healey is a local businessman. There are five other non executive members of the trust board: an academic with a health background; a retired industrial scientist; an administrator in further education; a chartered accountant in practice; and a prominent member of the local community with industrial links on the employee side.

In this hospital, a major concern which pervades all discussions and surfaces regularly in meetings is the matter of the acute services review being undertaken by the local health board. A major preoccupation of the non executives and of other groups is whether Healey will continue in its present form or whether the nearby general hospital (Hospital 'X') will assume some of its responsibilities. Nevertheless, despite such concerns the view of the non executives is that their presence has improved executive management. In the view of the non executives the executive team were not good at managing change, but they were now better at it.

Constraints

This perspective, that the non executives have brought a new sense of 'business' to this trust, is inhibited by a number of constraints on their activities. These constraints include:

- the relative positions of management *v* clinicians;
- the context in which the board has to operate;
- external influences on management practices; and
- the operation of the *quasi* market.

Management v clinicians

In relation to the relative positions of management *v* clinicians, the non executives reported 'language' difficulties with the medical terms and jargon, even though they had acquired some knowledge of medical protocols. This was exacerbated by the non executives' perceptions of the hospital consultants as being too dominant. In their view, there were too many clinicians, too few junior doctors. A consequence of this was 'less quantity and excess quality' in the words of one non executive board member. A further consequence was too much specialisation and a lack of flexibility with demarcation lines being created.

Context

As regards the context in which the board has to operate, the non executives had not been able to fulfil a strategic role. As one non executive stated:

We had an 'away day' to try to formulate strategy, but there is little that we can work on.

A consequence of the acute services review in this health board area was that their only strategic play was defensive, to delay. The acute services review was a major uncertainty. The non executives considered that there was a political dimension to this review. In this process they had discovered that they had less autonomy than they had thought.

External influences

In relation to external influences, a major negative influence, as perceived by non executive members of this board, was that of the NHS Management Executive. This influence operated at different levels. At one level, it is an issue of the location of nasty decisions. As one non executive commented:

The system has pushed the really hard decisions down to trusts where the opprobrium for poor service falls i.e. the real effects of the cuts. There has been negative press comment. This has been tackled, but it is always the bad rather than any good news.

More pointedly, at a more detailed level these non executives perceived an NHS Management Executive influence. One non executive stated:

We were guided forcibly by the executive management, who do not really seem to trust us, hence there are strong controls from the executive. We are puppets of the system. This is a huge constraint because we cannot look at the macro picture as it is not ours to look at.

Operation of the quasi market

There was considerable frustration within the non executive members of this board over the operation of the *quasi* market or internal market. The local health board was seen as having a huge, disproportionate, influence. It dominated the purchaser side of the split between purchaser and provider, with few GP fundholders in this area. The view of the board is that the health board is still operating 'as before'. The contractual negotiations were regarded as inefficient, time consuming and bureaucratic by this board. Indeed, one non executive director said:

> *There is a need for some strategic overview at a level lower than the NHS Management Executive, there are too many boards, at present. Also a greater need to liaise with social services.*

In terms of the Ferlie *et al* (1996) typology, this particular group of non executives has not moved much beyond Level A, the 'rubber stamp'. It has elements of Level B, the probing of the executive team, but local circumstances, the straitjacket of planning uncertainty, have prevented the further evolution of this particular team.

Conclusion

The Healey hospital management team have strived to bring a new dynamic to bear in the management of this hospital. This can be detected in a variety of ways. There are the various initiatives around the promulgation of best practice, and the formalisation of an explicit business strategy with explicit objectives for the trust. While there is a general view amongst the senior executives that the establishment of this hospital as a trust has been good for the quality of the management of the hospital, there are, nevertheless, significant constraints which impede the development of the senior executives into change agents. The most important of these is the review of acute hospital provision being conducted by the local health board, which has resulted in planning blight at Healey. There are also major frustrations here with relationships with the local health board, the contracting process in the internal market and the continuing drive for cash releasing efficiency savings from the health board as the agent of central government.

This tension between Healey hospital trust and its local health board was also evident from discussions with the clinical directors, who have been involved in contract negotiations with the health board. On their role within the hospital, evidence was gathered to the effect that, in general, good relations existed between the executive team and the clinical directors, although some reservations were stressed. An important dimension of these reservations was the attitude of these clinical directors to the financial management information which they received, with a mixed response: some had negative comments; some had positive experiences; some were critical of the content of the financial information which they received; and for some the critical factor was the person in the role of accountant explaining issues. In this way, this hospital has made moves to integrate clinicians within hospital management, but there is a potential for this to improve further.

Within this scenario, the non executive directors have sought to bring a new business awareness to the activities of the trust. In their view they have done so, in one significant area *ie* change management. Overall, however, the story of the non executive directors is depicted by feelings of frustration and limited impact on the steering of this hospital. It is evident that, within the non executive directors, there was dissatisfaction with the internal market, in general, and with the behaviour of the health board, in particular.

Overall, the use of accounting information within this hospital can be described as supportive. The challenges of meeting efficiency targets and the role of accounting in this are acknowledged by management. However, this is but one facet of the operation of a complex facility, the general hospital. In this respect, the financial framework within which this, and other, trusts operated (see table 1.4) was not seen as significant: these were financial constraints which had been met by the trust, to date, and were not the most dominant feature of the landscape in this hospital.

CHAPTER 3

MORGAN HOSPITAL

Background

Morgan hospital is a district general hospital. It employs over 1,000 staff, of whom over 60% are in medical, nursing and allied professions. It has 400 beds. In a typical year this hospital treats 15,252 in-patients, 6,415 day cases and 19,038 new out-patients. This hospital is located in an area of the country where there are few GP fundholders. The bulk of this Trust's income comes from contracts with its local health board. It also has contracts with other health boards and those GP fundholders in this area. As part of its contracting procedure, Morgan hospital has to meet specified, guaranteed waiting times for both general and specific procedures. Morgan's performance was 99% of patients within allocated time scales for general procedures and 100% of patients for specific procedures in 1997. We examine the views of the three parts of this hospital Trust's management, as follows: the executive team; the clinical directors; and non executive directors.

The executive team

In this hospital, the chief executive is a person with senior management experience in a variety of health care settings. Within this management team there are: a medical director; a director of nursing and quality; a director of human resources; and a director of finance. Most of these members of the executive have senior management experience from within the NHS.

The executive team at this hospital forms part of the management team. The management team includes the executive team members plus the clinical directors and some middle line directors. Both meet separately, the executive team meets weekly, and it meets with the management team twice per month. All the members of these teams have individual objectives and each clinical directorate has them as well. These objectives come about by discussion with the executive team and the management team decides whether it was reasonable to make these objectives.

In this management structure, the executive team was described by one member as being 'like a filter'. Plans come to the executive team in the first instance, for discussion. They then go on to the management team for further discussion and, if need be, to the trust board. Some of the ideas considered by these processes are generated internally, and some come from outside the Trust. The executive team sets priorities and, in this, any member may put items on to the team agenda. If these matters are of a strategic nature they are passed to the trust board.

The management of Morgan hospital is faced with three main pressures:

• the drive for cash releasing efficiency savings;
• relationships with the local health board; and
• developing marketing strategies.

Drive for cash releasing efficiency savings

Morgan has a clinical directorate system as discussed in the section on clinical directors. This is an attempt to move the focus of discussions away from the professionals to the directorates. A further mechanism to assist in this task is the creation of a 'forum', at which the executive team meets with a given clinical director and his team. Within this setting there is strong pressure put on clinical directors to meet their budgets. However, as one member of the executive team said, if these budget holders breach their budgets, they are not penalised. The executive team recognise that the forum is not quite working as intended. Nevertheless, they acknowledge that they have already squeezed out all of the easy savings. They are now confronted with moving on to making the kinds of cuts where quality of care is affected.

Relationships with the local health board

With regard to relationships with the local health board, there was dismay about contract negotiations as part of the internal market. This presents a picture of tension and confrontation. One member of the executive team described it as follows:

> ... there is an annual contracting cycle and we argue endlessly about money and activity. The power to change things is limited in the short term. For example, considering the services which we should introduce or withdraw, there are problems, partly because of bureaucracy and partly because of public expectations, so that shifting things quickly is very difficult. We need a long term strategy of changing things and in the short term we are just operating at the margin.

This story of conflict is reflected in the comments of other key players at Morgan: other members of the executive team; clinical directors; and non executive directors.

Developing marketing strategies

The executive team has addressed the development of marketing strategies by establishing closer links with local GP fundholding practices; entering other neighbouring health board areas to secure new markets for its services; and aligning itself with nearby, major teaching hospitals to rationalise its services and to provide useful career experience for medical and clinical staff. These combined strategies are still in their infancy, but they do demonstrate a senior management team which is willing to engage with the pressures of the market place.

In this hospital there was some disappointment expressed by the executive team about the realisation of the expected 'freedoms' arising from trust status but, overall, there is a positive response, as evidenced by this comment by a member of the executive team:

> ... trust status ... has affected this hospital positively. We have improved management decision making. We can make our own decisions rather than the health board making them for us. We are gradually working

our way through all information, for example, personnel records which
were previously set by the health board and we are changing these. It is
up to us what we do rather than the health board telling us what our
priorities should be, although they have tried to do this ...

In this scenario, explicit reference was made to the 'three card trick'
as a straitjacket. The 'three card trick' being the financial framework of
the specified return on capital employed, breaking even on revenue
account and staying within the external financing limit. It was also stated
that, at management team meetings, finance was always discussed as it
was a 'basic agenda item'.

Clinical directors

At this hospital there are only 40 consultants in all. Although
previously there were ten directorates, the directorate structure has been
streamlined (one for every specialism) and now there are only three. The
three directorates are: surgery; medical services; and clinical support. There
is a general perception amongst the clinical directors that access to top
management is good. A monthly meeting of all the consultants in the
hospital is valued by all involved and enables a spirit of collegiality. There
is an increased feeling of respect between management and the clinicians
which has been engendered by some quite rigorous employment contracts.
Overall there is an image of a small competent team running the hospital.

The relationship with management is very good, there's been a cleansing
exercise. I have a lot of confidence in management now. They have had
to compete and justify themselves and lots have been slung out. Clinical
directors aren't kept at a distance here. There's the executive director, the
medical director, three clinical directors, the management team and the
nursing managers. Really the main participants are the chief executive,
the finance director, the medical director and the three clinical directors,
we run the hospital. (CD1)

The interface of management and clinicians

There has been a recent new appointment of a finance director to the management team. This individual has been seen as highly influential. Through working hard to gain the trust of clinicians, the finance director has been able to establish himself as the sole representative of the Trust at contracting meetings with the health board. The argument has been that previous meetings were so confrontational that a new approach was required.

The dialogue has improved since the new finance director came, all contracting is now between him and the other finance director at the health board and no other person. He comes back to the team and reports, so it's all directed through the finance director which is a big improvement as he negotiates directly. Well, before they almost came to blows, it was a complete disaster. It's not the thing for clinicians to sit around a table discussing contracting .... Much depends on personalities, it does, we have a very strong finance director and a lot depends on strength of personality. We have a shortfall of funding in the coming financial year and the finance director has stated very strongly that all issues must go through him rather than going through the chief executive and then he will negotiate and report back in detail. Say we've negotiated on the basis of the delivery of 15,000 babies and it comes in at 15,500 well that's OK, but tonsils and hernias can be very variable and you need him to negotiate on them. (CD3).

At this site there are generally good working relationships both between the clinical directors and between the clinical directors and management. There is, however, evidence that the current finance director is emerging as a powerful figure in the Trust. Although this situation is accepted at the moment, in the future the clinical directors may begin to resent his dominance.

In terms of the clinical directors' management role within their directorates, two out of three of the directors favoured a rather directive approach, the third felt that peer pressure was usually enough for effective management although he would resort to sterner measures if peer pressure was not sufficient. The first two quotes below are illustrations from the views of the clinical directors who think that clinical directors should 'direct' their directorates. Although the first feels that this is successful, the second does not.

I now have authority over the nursing staff; there is one focus of attention and that's me. If there is a silly decision coming down the line on the nursing side now I can ward it off and that's good. Also I can go to say a couple of anaesthetists who aren't using theatre time properly and either they fall into line or I take it off them. There's one hand on the tiller now, before there were lots of people paddling. (CD1)

Take the clinical director quoted above he has authority over all theatres bar one so he is supposed to have the authority to decide if surgeons should have more or less lists and if they are operating enough but he doesn't say to a gynaecologist you are going to lose our list while we get the ENT contract sorted out. (CD2)

The third clinical director looked upon his role as being more of a 'supportive' than a 'directive' one.

I look upon being a clinical director as an exercise in support and guidance but, on occasion, the punitive component of the job becomes a necessity. Take job plans where areas are detailed and highlighted, well, where all the consultants are working in excess of contracted hours it does become harder to look at areas or you will lose goodwill. But really if individuals are not participating then peer pressure will prevail, that counts for more than anything a clinical director could do. (CD3)

The role of financial information

In part the more pivotal position described earlier for the new finance director has been achieved through delivering to the clinician directors financial information which relates to clinical activity and which yields some 'clear messages'. This is information they value and to which they can relate.

Historically we had very poor financial support with the previous finance director there was a lack of guidance to his staff on what clinicians need. Now we have excellent financial reporting systems, it even has sickness [absentee] levels in it. Of course it includes activity, predicted financial income related to activity, waiting time statistics and, oh, I can't remember what else is in it but it's a document which you can sit and look at and come away with clear messages. It was driven by our new finance director. He had realised at the Trust management meetings that there was a lack of ability in people to pick up on what was there in the financial information. (CD3)

The clinical directors' perceptions of financial information was that it has improved with the appointment of the new finance director. Previous to that it left much to be desired and there were still problems with identifying income and timeliness.

The financial information has been absolute and total rubbish but it is fast improving, we got rid of the last finance director and the new one has been much more successful. (CD1)

I've become accustomed to a lack of financial information. You have to understand the way the minds of finance people work and it has taken me a long time. This idea that you have got to balance your books at the end of the year. If you work out how they work then you can get improvements but you have to keep pressing for activity data and income as well. But the finance people keep regressing to just expenditure, that your budget is just your expenditure budget. (CD2)

The relationship with the health board

As in all the other case study sites the interface between the Trust and the health board was a difficult and conflictual one although as discussed above, at this site this has been very recently 'solved' by locating the finance director as the sole negotiator.

The relationship with the health board hasn't been terribly amicable of late. Recently the health board and the Trust have been completely unable to come to any arrangement. The health board believes that negotiation means not moving from a pre-determined position, they have no conception of trying to get to a win-win situation. There is also a personality issue and, basically, we are not feeling terribly happy with each other. (CD2)

Well there are problems with the health board. Our health board still thinks that they are running the hospital. We appointed six new consultants and there was all hell to play at the health board, it's none of their business. The health board has a capped budget but they have to play the game. If they don't purchase enough then our waiting lists go up and that's the health board's problem, it shows that they just aren't purchasing enough. (CD1)

Non executive directors

At Morgan hospital, there are six non executive board members. The chairman at Morgan is retired. He formerly worked in the commercial sector. There are five other members of the board; an industrialist with significant experience of senior management; an industrialist with local government experience; an academic who lives in the local community; a retired person who previously had a significant involvement in health related charitable work; and a member who had administrative experience within the NHS and in charities. At this hospital, the chairman is highly visible and active in management matters. His commitment to the trust is such that the time which he spends in the hospital exceeds his formal obligation. Other members of the non executives are also in the hospital a great deal.

The major focus of the chairman in this trust has been on the reorganisation of this hospital's management. This has resulted in significant changes at the senior executive level of management in the board, with the following new appointments during his tenure as chairman: chief executive; director of finance; director of nursing; and director of human resources. The need for such replacements at the senior level was seen by the chairman as the need to address major management problems. However, while the role of the chairman can be seen as adding a new business awareness, it is notable that all of the replacements for these posts were persons who were already employed in the health service.

The above reorganisation of the management team has absorbed a great deal of the chairman and non executives' time. This has deflected the board from the pursuit of a strategy for the trust. This was described as being 'on the back burner because of management problems'. However, the trust board is now addressing this issue. There are constraints on the development of an effective strategy at this board, some of which are situational. For example, it was pointed out that attracting hospital consultants in certain specialities can be difficult at this trust. Factors in this may be location and the limited opportunities for hospital consultants to undertake private work at this hospital. Nevertheless, the trust board has supported the initial strategy of the executive team to expand into neighbouring health boards to gain patients and collaborate with the nearest teaching hospitals to maximise services and specialities on offer.

In providing the oversight function at this trust, the experiences of the chairman and his non executives reveal signs of frustration at their inability to act with as much freedom as they would wish. This frustration stems from two sources: the NHS Management Executive; and the local health board. On dealings with the NHS Management Executive, the chairman said:

> We are doing the NHS Management Executive's dirty work …. . We have had problems with the management executive on the appointment of certain replacements. They wanted their man and sought undue influence.

However, the above difficulties are of less significance than the tensions between this hospital trust and its health board. There have been clashes between the chairman of this trust and the chairman of the health board. The non executives of this hospital trust challenge the ability of the local health board to function effectively. Views expressed by these and other non executives suggested that the health board role is out of date, and that there are not enough GP fundholders in the market, either.

The contracting process is absorbing a lot of resources and for what benefit? A positive hindrance. And it is costly to do. And the annual cycle of contract setting is too short.

This group of non executives saw the way forward as the demise of the existing number of health boards with some rationalisation of their numbers and activities. In terms of their internal activities, despite the above management changes, they saw themselves as well served with financial and other reports to discharge their duties. Also, at the Board, the lack of specific medical knowledge of non executive members was not seen as a problem as the medical director and the nursing director were there to guide and sift out problems and, at a higher level, to advise on prioritisation.

Overall, this group of non executives does not fall within Level A of the Ferlie *et al* (1996) typology of hospital boards. It is not a rubber stamp, having replaced most of its full time executive team over a relatively short period of time. At the chairman level, the non executive extends beyond Level B, substantial involvement in strategic prioritisation, although certain of these decisions may be more operational than strategic. This shows a determination to bring new business values to bear in the operation of this hospital trust.

Conclusion

At Morgan hospital there has been a new dynamic in the senior management of this trust. The impetus, however, for much of this dynamic derives from the initiatives taken by the chairman of this trust to seek the replacement of several senior executives: chief executive; director of finance; director of nursing; and director of human resources. However the mechanisms adopted by this executive team are more of the consensual variety, than the confrontational. An exception to this is the establishment of the forum at which clinical directors are held accountable for their financial and non financial performance by the executive team. However, it is acknowledged that this is still in its infancy and is not yet operating effectively. Nevertheless, the Morgan executive team has made a start on the appraisal and pursuit of market opportunities.

On the issue of devolving managerial responsibilities to clinical directors to achieve a greater integration of clinicians within hospital management, Morgan has made some advances. However, to achieve advances it has dispensed with the services of five clinical directors and re-grouped around the three remaining clinical directors. While the three remaining clinical directors now report favourably upon management matters, there is an inconsistency here ie they have been removed from the significant management process of negotiating contracts and welcome this reduction in their management commitment. There appears to be some more favourable response to different styles of financial reports, but what is crucial here is their response to financial events (eg deficits within their directorates) and how the clinical directors respond to these.

There are, within this trust, some elements of a new business awareness, mainly at the chairman level. However, much of this chairman's focus has been a greater preoccupation with the operational, rather than the strategic side of things. There are expressions of frustration from these non executives over the nature of their role and with the hospital trust's dealings with the outside world, notably the health board and the NHS Management Executive.

Overall, within this hospital trust, there is considerable significance attached to financial matters, although reservations have been expressed by various of these key actors over the quality of financial information. There was also concern expressed at this trust at the financial straitjacket of the hospital trust financial regulation framework.

CHAPTER 4

TALBOT HOSPITAL

Background

Talbot hospital is a major teaching hospital. It treats over 200,000 patients in a typical year. It employs approximately 2,400 (whole time equivalent) staff with some 1,500 of these in the clinical areas. Within the ranks of its clinical staff it has many eminent authorities within their specialisms. This fact is underlined by the substantial research funding that this hospital trust has attracted, in addition to its NHS funding. The local health board is the main purchaser of the services of this hospital trust (at 75% of all referrals). However, a further 20% of this trust's referrals come from other health boards, showing the importance of this hospital's service on a supra regional basis. Some 4% of the purchases of this hospital trust's services are also made by GP fundholders. We examine the perceptions of the three strands of this hospital's management, as follows: the executive team; the clinical directors; and non executive directors.

The executive team

The executive team at Talbot hospital is headed by a chief executive with considerable NHS experience. In the chief executive's management team there are: a director of finance; a medical director; and a director of nursing and quality, all of whom have had substantial experience of the NHS gained at this and other hospital sites. Within the executive team there is a mix of public and private sector experience, some of which is extensive.

This management team has brought a new dynamic to the management of this trust. Some of the pressures for this dynamic are external, but the internal response has been that of a management keen to engage with these pressures. There are outward signs of this new management evidenced by the formal statement of individual objectives and their appraisal and, at the corporate level, by the formulation of corporate objectives and an explicit business strategy. There is also a definite hierarchy for the addressing of issues as shown in Figure 4.1.

Figure 4.1: Management structure at Talbot hospital

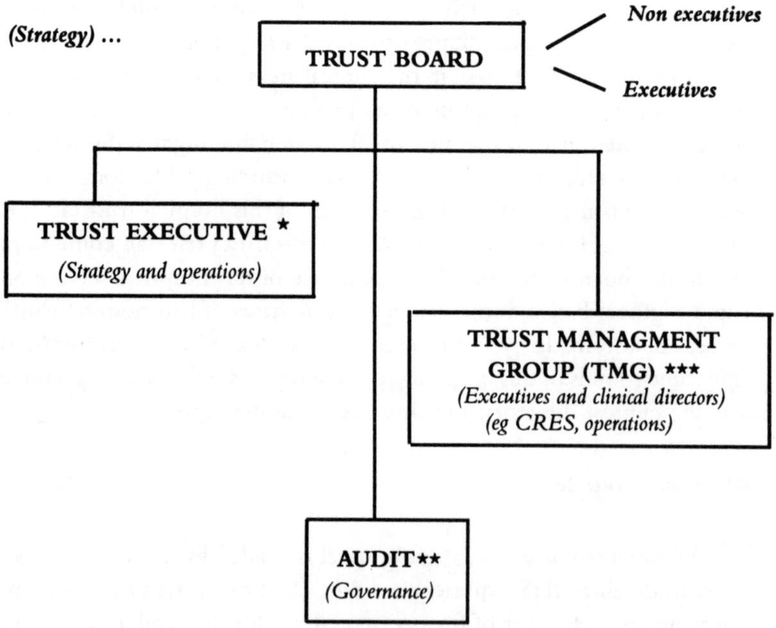

(Strategy) ...

TRUST BOARD

Non executives

Executives

TRUST EXECUTIVE *
(Strategy and operations)

TRUST MANAGMENT GROUP (TMG) ***
(Executives and clinical directors)
(eg CRES, operations)

AUDIT**
(Governance)

*   meets once a week; every 6 weeks meets with a clinical director and his team, examine accounts and forecast.
**   meets once every 3/4 months, formal sub-committee reports to Board, internal and external audit.
***   meets once per month.

There are a number of major issues which have dominated management's actions at Talbot hospital in recent times. These include the continuing pressure to review all acute activities in line with the shift of emphasis to community care and the management of hospital resources, particularly in the context of gaining contracts for health care services and the need to generate cash releasing efficiency savings.

There have been difficulties caused by the supra regional specialities offered by this hospital. In present circumstances, there are difficulties over tertiary referrals for such services, with different health boards taking different attitudes to the purchase of these services. The chief executive has argued for a more careful evaluation of supra regional specialisms by the three health boards concerned. However, while this issue is of undoubted importance to the management and to the future of this hospital trust, the issue of hospital resource management represents the most fundamental, continual issue in the daily management of the trust hospital. There are two aspects to this: contract setting in the internal market; and the need to identify cash releasing efficiency savings.

Contract setting in the internal market

In relation to contract setting in the internal market, there is a widespread scepticism within the management of this trust of the current arrangements in contracting for services with health boards, as the following comments by senior executives illustrate:

The split of purchaser and provider hasn't worked in the sense of the market. The market isn't operating, money doesn't follow patients, the split of purchaser and provider is characterised by purchasers who don't understand what they are purchasing ... and

Contracting is very time consuming. There is also a major practical problem. No matter where you signed up to increased activity you never got the relevant income. Our medical guys are worried about that. One of our biggest frustrations is in the contracting process where

you are coming up against people who aren't authorised to actually conclude deals or give you anything and this could change when it went back to the health board level ...

The above typify the comments of the management: the frustrations of being locked into an annual cycle of contested contracts which are the subject of intense negotiation, but, more importantly, which threaten to destabilise planning at the trust because of the short term focus of the planning cycle.

The need to identify cash releasing efficiency savings

On the need to identify and generate cash releasing efficiency savings, we see the principal means by which accounting is used as a lever for change in this organisation. As one senior executive stated:

This ... is on the agenda all the time.

This annual imperative to achieve cash savings has persisted for over a decade. There is concern within the executive team that, while in the early days it was possible to identify such savings, now the impact of these savings targets is impacting on services, with the reduction of service capability included for consideration as a possible means of making savings. One mechanism introduced by the executive team is that of clinical directorates, with specified clinicians assuming budgetary responsibility for their speciality. The operation of this scheme is discussed in the section on clinical directors. It is important, however, to obtain a management perspective on what this scheme is achieving currently and what its potential is. The concept of clinical directorates is one which had been deployed at this hospital before it received trust status. In its earlier forms, however, the clinical directors did not have significant budgetary responsibility. Last year (1997) was the first year of devolved budgets to clinical directors. The advent of these budgets has helped to bring about a more corporate focus, rather than the pursuit of individual aims on the part of the directorates. This, in itself represents a significant shift, in the view of the management. However, the management are aware that some of these clinical directors are more responsive than others in delivering on the corporate aims. These issues are discussed more fully in the section on clinical directors.

In the view of this management team the NHS is dogged by one particular situation namely *we have limited resources, how do we prioritise?* In addressing this situation the management expressed the view that trust status helps, particularly in the deployment of capital and employment policies. However, while there is a sense of a business awareness being instilled in this hospital trust, it is important not to overstate the case. As one member of the executive team whose previous experience is entirely that of the private sector stated, working in the hospital trust was significantly different from any private sector organisation in which he had worked.

Clinical directors

The clinical directorate structure is devolved and there are a number of clinically based directorates. Not surprisingly in the context of these multiple groups there is some diversity of opinion between the clinical directors regarding their relationship with management. Views range from,

> *Management have lost the heart, soul and mind of the clinicians. (CD1)*

to

> *We as a group, the clinical directors, get on with management well, actually that's silly isn't it because we are management, I mean that we get on with the next level, there are no fundamental problems. (CD2)*

We examine the views of clinical directors in three stages:

- the interface between management and clinicians;
- clinical directors' views on the role of financial information; and
- the hospital trust relationship with the health board.

The interface between management and clinicians

Positive comments *vis-à-vis* the interface with management were expressed over 'being listened to' and over the accessibility of management within the hospital.

Personally, I think that at this trust we have good working relationships within the clinical directors as a group and between us and the executive, we are listened to. (CD8)

The chief executive does take an interest and tries to interact. People appreciate just seeing the executive management in the department. The chief executive comes and joins in meetings once or twice a year, that's important to people, he asks people if they want to ask questions and that really makes a difference to them. (CD6)

Clinical directors were also aware of the opportunities afforded by the directorate system to engage with management agendas.

I believe in the principle of clinical directorates, doctors have to be involved in management, if we aren't we have only got ourselves to blame. (CD8)

Well for years and years we moaned that we didn't have a management role and we thought that we could do it better than non medical management did. We have certainly had our bluff called and it is useful to get a flavour for the problems and the degree of executive authority is very useful but it can be a cumbrous system having managers who aren't really managers and managers. (CD6)

Where concerns were voiced over the interface with non medical management, the three main areas focused on were:

- a perception that management do not understand or are disconnected from clinical activities;
- that management are only reactive rather than alert to market opportunities; and
- that management keep the clinical directors at arm's length.

On non medical management's lack of insight into clinical activities and the interests of patients the following comments were expressed:

Management are disengaged from service delivery, they say how much does this cost and they ask what is length of stay and how can we get it down, they don't think of what this means for the patient. (CD8)

There is a lack of insight into the clinical management of disease processes and management fail to recognise important developments. Cutting back and saving money, this is management's only focus. (CD1)

On the other hand some clinical directors felt that this differential focus was inevitable and it was the responsibility of the clinical directors to 'fight their corner' or to educate management. For example, CD2 expressed reservations over the finance director's 'break-even' mentality.

A complimentary view was that the clinical directors also had to accept responsibility to understand the perspective of management.

But the clinical directors haven't truly understood the difficulties that the executive face and so we are intolerant. If we understood their problems we would have more sympathy for the way in which they have to say 'No' to us ... more openness, more frankness, that's what's necessary. For example, if the clinical directors understood the difficulties the trust faces in its negotiations with X health board. (CD3)

On the perceived strengths and weaknesses of management, one clinical director commented:

Management aren't accountable and it's not clear who is accountable for any decision. It is the responsibility of management to do some managing, all they do is respond to crises, they have no feel for clinical needs. (CD1)

Although management were considered to have a good feel for the more 'marketable' services at the trust.

I think that the managers here have a good understanding of the marketability of certain clinical skills; they certainly understand that we are leading edge in tertiary services, they see those as big plus points, oh,

> *yes, they are very encouraging on that front. They are less knowledgeable on how the place works on a day to day basis but that's not really their fault. (CD6)*

The most widely held view on the interface with management was that the clinical directors were kept at arm's length. One clinical director expressed this as follows:

> *At the moment we are kept at arm's length, now in no other business would this happen, we are the income generators, we bring in the money, we should be at the top table. (CD5)*

The perception is that the present management structure can in effect exclude the clinical directors from strategic decision making.

> *The executives think that they have maintained the right to run the trust as they think fit, they formed other groups, such as the trust strategy group, to which the clinical directors weren't party, and so there was little clinical director input. (CD3)*

> *One comment I would make, though, is that sometimes one does feel that the trust management group discusses and doesn't decide and then when the trust executive group meets then they decide. In that forum there is only one clinician, the medical director, I'm not saying that we all need to be there but only one out of eleven isn't much. I think it would be better if there were two or three clinical voices. (CD8)*

One clinical director commented that management knew that the clinical directors, as a group, were dissatisfied with their lack of input into the management process.

> *The clinical directors do get dissatisfied, the chief executive said to me recently that he knew that we wished that we had more teeth, more autonomy. For instance, last year it did get a bit nasty, we talked about cash releasing efficiency savings and it was all very confidential and theoretical and then the next thing I knew I was expected to sign redundancy letters. Of course, I didn't do it. (CD4)*

The role of financial information

The clinical directors would like more transparency over overheads and more information which links with clinical activities. On overheads, clinicians are keenly aware of the burden of central costs and would welcome further information on allocations.

I have an income of £18m but I have a budget of half that. A huge chunk of money is top sliced to cover everything from the chief executive's salary to lighting the building. (CD2)

I'd like an income and expenditure sheet that is meaningful and I don't get that. I get to spend less than half of our real income. (CD3)

I don't understand where the overheads come from and they are a huge amount, 50%. How do they choose what to put into overheads? Really half my budget is unaccounted for. (CD6)

Clinicians only find financial information meaningful when it is linked with their activities and, therefore, has the potential to be used to improve clinical practice.

We have costs of total numbers of examinations per bed holding directorate but we need more specific information like numbers of specific types of examination per individual doctor. We would be able to work out who might be abusing the system and then we could look at that. (CD6)

You can get detailed information on the costs of drugs and pharmacy, you can see that we have spent so many thousands on a specific drug, you can just look at the prescribing lists. But you can't get information on practices. For example, most of the theatres come out of the surgical budget but there are two theatres which don't and the finance people can't say who pays for these theatres. We have global figures and so we can't identify the costs of procedures. (CD1)

Linking budgets to outputs rather than inputs was recognised as the way forward but moving beyond outputs to outcomes was difficult. Furthermore clinicians and managers can have differing views on what constitutes an 'outcome'.

Budgets should look at outputs, that's important and appropriate and clinical directors should be shaping the factors on which the budget is founded. But, of course, outcomes are difficult, you can measure death, that's easy to measure but other outcomes aren't ... Managers do think differently, take PFI, managers see that as completing a process, as a final outcome, but we see it as improving quality of care and as making a viable hospital. We see PFI as part of a process rather than an outcome. (CD5)

The relationship with the health board

The relationship with the health board was almost universally described by the clinical directors as confrontational, as the following comment illustrates:

The trust meets the health board, well, really it's a case of the trust confronts the health board. The health board, they are really a bunch of acronyms with money. (CD3)

The main specific complaints against the health board were that they were 'uninformed' purchasers and that they were unwilling to take responsibility for cutting services, as characterised by the following observation:

They don't have the professional knowledge so as purchasers they, the health board, have unreasonable expectations. Also they are bullet shy, they have no view on which services to cut. (CD5)

The answer to the dilemma of the 'uninformed' purchaser was thought to lie either in imparting expertise, as illustrated by the following comment:

You would have to have brighter people in the health board, people with experience of providing more motivated people who have been educated in the modern era. As it is what we have are medical advisers with a public health/occupational medicine background. But maybe doctors of this sort, to assist purchasers, don't exist. (CD7) or in gradually diminishing the role of the health board, as the following statement indicates:

I think that the health board will assume a smaller and smaller role. I think that they will disappear as commissioners, I hope so anyway because they are a pain. What's the point of them if they aren't purchasing health care? (CD2)

Non executive directors

At the Talbot hospital there have been attempts by the non executive board members to bring a business awareness to the management of this hospital, but their contribution has had a limited success. The chairman of this trust is a person with significant experience of the world of business and he has made a major contribution to the setting of this trust's strategy. He has an active dialogue with the senior executives. The chairman has been very supportive of development initiatives at this hospital. There are four other non executive members of this board: a senior manager at director level of a major public company; another manager, at director level, of a major company; a retired teacher with social work experience; and a person who had major experience of charitable work in the health sector.

However, the non executive members of the board with significant business experience other than the chairman have made less of an impact. This is not a question of their ability to contribute but of the time available to them and the context within which non executive directors operate. On the time available non executive directors with less pressing business commitments are more available and appear to shoulder a disproportionate amount of non executive board member work. More importantly, on the context within which non executive directors operate, the expected role of the non executive members of the board has not materialised, as envisaged. As table 1.2 sets out, there was a declared role for non executives of determining the overall policies of the trust. This implies a distinct role at the strategic level. However, despite the fact that this trust has been engaged heavily in major strategic activities, including involvement in a major acute services review in this health board area, the non executives have not considered themselves to be involved sufficiently in matters strategic. A general comment echoed the views at other trusts that the non executive members were unable to address any real strategic issues. They had expected to be able to. In their view, the health board had not come off the fence and issued any clear strategies, and it was also inconsistent. As a consequence they did not know where they were going as a trust. As a result, the trust's strategy was limited to meeting ever increasing and blanket cost cuts. This was seen by them all as frustrating.

The above perspective, of frustration with the impact of oversight agencies, such as the health board, clearly influences the previous observations about a lack of a strategic role for the non executives. There are other dimensions on this theme which lend support to this attenuation of the role of the non executive directors. One non executive expressed concern about their counterparts at health boards. In his view, the non executive members of health boards seemed remote from the everyday life of the hospital trust. For example, they never seemed to visit the trusts. This caused concern about the ability of such non executives at health board level to make informed decisions about the trusts in their area.

· Another manifestation of this frustration with their role as non executives was expressed vis-à-vis the NHS Management Executive. As the chairman of this trust stated:

> ... the Management Executive are always encouraging the trust to take risks and push out the frontiers, but the whole system mitigates against this being possible. It cannot be done because trusts cannot borrow or build up reserves and are constrained tightly, in financial terms. Any unsuccessful venture would result in loss and hence, either, at best, the loss of savings made elsewhere or the failure to meet external financing limit and other financial targets. The downside outweighs the upside. Hence, there is no incentive or mechanism to encourage 'pushing out the frontiers...

In this trust, the behaviour of these non executives is not that of Level A, the 'rubber stamp' in Ferlie et al's (1996) typology. It is closer to Level B, in which the non executives probe and question the executives.

Indeed, the chief executive acknowledges the ability of his non executives to ask penetrating questions. However, in the case of the chairman, this trust typifies Level C, in which there appears to be a substantial involvement in strategic options. The executive team and the chief executive, in particular, are sensitive to the need to involve non executive members of the trust board in strategic matters. Indeed, these non executives recognise a business awareness within this hospital trust, a change from former, more bureaucratic forms of management. But, to the extent that this exists, it is a manifestation of the behaviour of the executive team and, to some extent, the influence of the chairman.

Conclusion

In conclusion, the management of this hospital trust can be depicted as bringing a dynamic to its appraising of its opportunities, the enhancement of areas of noted expertise, and in re-shaping its priorities, in the context of tight financial constraints. A related issue is the devolution of budgets to hospital doctors as clinical directors. While there are signs of some acceptance of this role by clinicians there is also evident tension around this activity. In many ways, this is not unexpected, particularly given the history of attempts to implement budgets for clinicians. This response, of tension and, at best, mixed acceptance, is not a criticism of the management of this trust, but the revelation of deep seated attitudes amongst clinicians in favour of more patient care and against financial restrictions. In this sense, these new arrangements have not yet integrated these senior clinicians within the hospital management. The executive team are aware of this particular challenge.

Also, there is evidence within this trust of a new business awareness. While a contribution to this has come from the activities of the chairman, particularly at the strategic level, the other non executives have made less of an impact. In many ways, their experience of their role as non executives was one of frustration. To the extent that a business awareness exists within this trust, this is more an issue of an impetus derived from the executive team, particularly the chief executive, rather than the non executive directors, with the notable exception of the chairman.

In this world of the hospital trust, accounting has assumed an important, perhaps a dominant role. However, this significance is not a product of the financial framework of breaking even on revenue account, earning 6% on capital employed and staying within the external financing limit (see table 1.4 in chapter 1) which is achievable, but seen as remote from the management of the hospital. Instead, accounting takes on a significance in the context of the contracting process, in measuring income generation, and in the cash releasing efficiency savings targets, in identifying cost savings. In this way accounting assumes a major role: a constraint on the management of the hospital which cannot be ignored.

CHAPTER 5

CONCLUSION

This study has investigated the management of self governing hospital trusts which were created as part of the NHS reforms (DOH, 1989). These trusts were established as providers in the internal market for health care. This study raises serious questions about the efficacy of the internal market. Specifically, these findings revealed flaws in the operation of the market, which undermined its potential efficient operation. These arrangements also reveal weaknesses in accountability relationships in the split between purchaser and provider. Also, the drive for cash releasing efficiency savings has placed accounting at the centre of the drive for cost savings in hospital trusts. This circumstance has posed serious challenges, both for accounting for management and also for the management of such reductions in resources. Key issues arising from the case studies included in this project were the following:

• the impact of accounting on the management of trust hospitals;
• the operation of the market, notably the efficacy of the split between purchaser and provider;
• the adequacy of the financial framework for hospital trusts;
• the effectiveness of clinical directorates in the hospital trusts;
• the role of non executive directors of trust boards;
• hospital management: over or under resourced? and
• the future of hospital trusts.

The impact of accounting on the management of trust hospitals

It might be expected that the extension of devolved budgetary control systems to, and within, hospital trusts (particularly to clinical directors) represents the most likely manner in which accounting impacts on the management of hospitals. The evidence of these case studies, however, reveals that the most direct manner in which accounting practices have impacted on the management of the hospital trusts included in this study has been *via* cash releasing efficiency savings (CRES). These are given to each hospital, as part of the process of its negotiations for contracts with purchasers (health boards, principally the local health board). These operate as a device by which hospital trusts are given a nominal amount for services purchased which is then deflated by a fixed percentage, currently 3%, as an expected 'efficiency gain'. This is a system which has prevailed, in a variety of different guises, in the health service since the 1980s. The immediate effect of those CRES targets is the elimination, or the virtual elimination of any increase allowed for inflation. If this consequence is combined with increased activity levels, fuelled by, amongst other things, central government initiatives to reduce waiting lists, it can be seen that the drive for cash releasing efficiency savings heightens the awareness and significance of accounting information. Of particular concern, here are the reported effects whereby the management of the hospital trusts included in this study all reported that the identification of such cost savings over such a prolonged period of time had eroded the obvious targets where savings could be made and now the impacts were resulting in delicate and difficult decisions which impacted on the quality of care at these hospitals. This is a matter of extreme delicacy for the management of these hospitals and has resulted in the rationalisation of facilities *eg* temporary or permanent closure of wards, the reduction of staff (labour is the highest cost component), and the reduction in routine maintenance. This entire aspect of the funding of hospital activity, its implications, and consequences for the quality of care merits further detailed study as a matter of extreme importance.

The operation of the market

This study has demonstrated major reservations over the efficacy of the internal market. A key mechanism in the internal market was the creation of the split between purchaser and provider, with the hospital trusts as providers of health care and the purchasers of health care such as the health boards and the GP fundholders. However, these three case studies were sited in health boards where there was little competition. The local health board was a virtual monopoly purchaser of services from local monopsonies, which undermines the concept of the split between purchaser and provider in the market.

Furthermore, the mechanisms of the split between purchaser and provider present important accountability issues. The basis upon which purchases of health care are agreed is that of contracts. Contracts are arrived at by a process of negotiation. However, the experiences of the providers in this study, all of whom provide health care in different health board areas, suggest that this contracting process is flawed on the following counts:

• currently contracting is based on an annual cycle which mitigates against planning;
• all kinds of care are treated in the same manner, whereas at least some merit longer term contracts;
• the contracting process has become intense and confrontational;
• there is a lack of sophistication in contract setting, with little movement away from the 'block' style contracts; and
• the focus of contract negotiation is predominantly on costs and funding, with a lack of consideration of the quality of care.

The major effects of the above dimensions of the contracting process are those of tense, conflict ridden exchanges, rather than a more considered evaluation of strategies for health care. There is a consequent emphasis on the short term which destabilises planning within hospital trusts, which have considerable investment, with considerable fixed costs. These findings represent the situation in the Scottish health service. However, in other parts of the UK there are provider hospitals in monopsony situations. There is also the potential of a dominant role being assumed by health authorities, the English equivalent of health boards.

Adequacy of the financial framework for hospital trusts

The creation of hospital trusts has attracted criticism because of the prominence given to finance and accounting numbers. A major source of this potential importance is the financial framework which regulates the activities of hospital trusts. As part of this study, we examined the efficacy of the three part financial framework:

*   the requirement to break even on revenue account;
*   the specified target return on capital employed of 6%; and
*   the external financing limit (EFL) which placed a constraint on borrowing levels of trusts.

In the three hospital trusts included in this study, these three constraints were always met. One of these hospital's management expressed concern about the 'straitjacket' which this three part framework created for the trust, but this was primarily frustration at the borrowing constraint. However, this was not a general picture within the management of these hospitals. These targets were met by these trusts. They did not loom large in the thinking of the senior management groups included in this study. Indeed, in our view, this structure seems over determined, with the highly specific target return on capital employed implying a degree of precision which is unrealistic. A more meaningful approach would be a system of negotiation which permitted a range of predetermined returns on capital employed, with a relaxation of the external financing limit, although this latter aspect of the regulatory framework is crucially dependant on the future of the Private Finance Initiative.

The effectiveness of clinical directorates

The idea of clinical directorates is that a management structure is created in which clinicians have a clearly defined role with explicit financial responsibilities. Historically, this has been an area of contention within hospitals, with a succession of failed initiatives. Within these case studies, the clinical directorates have been established, but have been tinkered with, by executive management, usually by reducing the numbers of clinical directors. The executive teams at the case study settings had sought to involve these clinicians in the contracting process with their local health boards. This had caused concern in at least two of these trusts that the fractious confrontations and the time consuming negotiations were de-motivating those clinicians who had been prepared to become clinical directors. Within the clinical directors included in this study there were mixed responses to the use of financial information, with reservations expressed over the nature and the manner in which it was being provided to the clinical directors. However, it must be noted at the time of the case study visits the clinical directorates with devolved financial responsibilities were in their infancy. In this respect, this particular initiative merits continued support as a possible means of achieving an integration of hospital doctors within the management of their trusts.

The role of non executive board members

This study has shown that while the non executive members of these trust boards have sought to bring a new business awareness to hospital trusts their impact has been limited. In this regard, there is a distinction between the contributions of the chairmen of these trust boards and the other non executives. The chairmen of these trust boards have all had significant influence on the conduct and operation of the management of these hospitals. However, the general picture emerges of frustration with the role of the non executive. A major aspect of this was the lack of a role in strategic matters. To some extent this was a function of the short termism of the internal market which was accentuated by the existence of acute hospital services reviews by their local health boards. However, the non executives included in this study had a strong sense of commitment to their local trusts and often spent greater time at the hospital than was formally required of them. Given the relatively novel nature of these trust boards, a further period to examine the wider potential of the non executives is merited. In particular, new forms of governance and accountability to local communities and to financiers may be necessary.

Hospital management

In the case study settings, the executive management teams were predominantly persons with NHS rather than private sector experience. There was reported evidence of proactive behaviour by these management teams in changing and making more effective the management of these hospitals. There was a general view within these management teams that, whilst the original concept of the devolved 'freedoms', which were to be given to trust management had not been realised, they had nevertheless made significant improvements to management practices arising from trust status. The major benefit was the ability to make decisions more quickly by hospital management. The activities of the trust executive teams were heavily constrained, however, by the following:

• the operation of the internal market;
• the incidence of acute hospital services reviews;
• the nature of contractual agreements, in particular cash releasing efficiency saving stipulations; and
• adversarial positions between these trusts and their local health boards.

Hospital management has been the subject of intense criticism to the effect that its costs are excessive and that this is a drain on the tight fundholding regimes of hospital trusts. However, given the size and complexity of these undertakings, *prima facie*, this does not appear to be the case. The management teams interviewed as part of this study were highly motivated in the pursuit of their trust's goals, despite the pressures to achieve them. One senior executive commented:

It is a shame that we have become a political football. The media monitor everything and health is such a big issue. We have so many pressures on us to improve access and quality and they simultaneously push up costs. And all the time the media is watching and we are in the public eye.

The future of hospital trusts

The creation of hospital trusts has resulted in considerable critical commentary. However, many of such criticisms need to be disentangled from a range of influences, which have impacted on the everyday experiences of these hospitals. There have been significant external pressures, for example, the nature of the market, the pressures to make cost savings and wider issues including reviews of acute hospital services, which have had significant effects on the activities of those hospitals. In this study, the managements of these hospital trusts have grappled with these pressures and continued to strive to provide the best patient care which they can achieve for the populations which they serve. The case studies in this investigation show the potential of such hospital trusts to identify with local communities and be responsive to their health care needs. What is critical in obtaining the best results for the management of the Scottish hospital service is not that of the management of hospital trusts, which this study shows to be robust, even if in need of refinement, but minimising the turbulence of the internal market in health care.

In this respect, the most recent White Paper (Scottish Office, 1997) on the future of the NHS in Scotland signals the end of the internal market, such as it was, and this research supports this policy change. Nevertheless, there remain major issues for the efficient and effective organisation and delivery of health care which this research report identifies. Most importantly, these include:

- the need for more effective coordination of planning, although the proposed framework in the 1997 White Paper, *op. cit.* has overtones of the purchaser/provider split of the internal market;
- the preservation of the hospital trusts as small, responsive organisations, which runs counter to their proposed aggregation by the government into larger, more bureaucratic units;
- the need to achieve more means of controlling the management of financial resources in trusts than by CRES which is an inefficient, blunt instrument;

- the opportunity to work within the proposed freedoms when these trusts were first established, but which were never realised in practice because of continuing central government intervention; and
- the need to resolve inter-professional conflicts by providing settings, such as small scale responsive trusts, which promote communication and coordination between executives, health care professionals and non executives and their local communities.

If these dimensions of trusts are preserved or enhanced, there is the opportunity to build on the successful experiences of the last reform of the NHS, without the tensions and difficulties of the so called market. If these considerations are not taken into account in the current reorganisation of the NHS, there is a danger of replacing the iniquities of the market with the inefficiencies of centralised bureaucracies.

REFERENCES

Ashburner, L (1993) *The Composition of NHS Trust Boards: A National Perspective*, pp.16-39, in E.Peck and P.Spurgeon (eds) NHS Trusts in Practice, Longman.

Appleby, J, R Robinson, W Ranade, V Little, and J Slater, (1990) 'The Use of Markets in the Health Service: The NHS Reforms and Managed Competition', *Public Money & Management*, Vol.10, No.4, pp.27-34.

Department of Health and Social Security (DHSS)(1985) *Management Budgeting*, Circular HN(85)3, DHSS, London.

Department of Health and Social Security (DHSS)(1986) *Resource Management*, Circular HN(86)34, DHSS, London.

Department of Health (DOH)(1989a) *Working for Patients*, HMSO.

Department of Health (DOH)(1989b) *Working for Patients*, Self governing Hospitals, Working Paper No.1.

Denzin, N K (1978) *The Research Act* (2nd edition) McGraw-Hill.

Enthoven, A (1985) *Reflections on the Management of the National Health Service*, Nuffield Provincial Hospitals Trust.

Ferlie, E, L Fitzgerald and L Ashburner, (1996) 'Corporate Governance in the Post 1990 NHS: The Role of the Board', *Public Money & Management*, April-June, 1996, pp.15-21.

Giddens, A (1984) *The Constitution of Society*, Polity Press, Cambridge.

Griffiths, R (1983) *NHS Management Enquiry* (The Griffiths Report), DHSS.

Kaplan, R S (1986) 'The Role for Empirical Research in Management Accounting', *Accounting, Organizations & Society*, Vol.11, pp.429-452.

King, M, I Lapsley, F Mitchell and J Moyes (1994a) 'Costing Needs and Practices in a Changing Environment: The Potential for ABC in the NHS', *Financial Accountability & Management*, May, 1994, Vol.10, No.2, pp.143-160.

King, M, I Lapsley, F Mitchell and J Moyes (1994b) *Activity-based Costing in Hospitals: A Case Study Investigation*, CIMA.

Lapsley, I (1990) 'Accounting for Public Sector Capital - The National Health Service', *The Accountant's Magazine*, August, pp.45-51.

Lapsley, I (1993) 'Markets, Hierarchies and the Regulation of the National Health Service', *Accounting & Business Research*, No.91A, pp.384-393.

Lapsley, I (1994, 1997) 'Market Mechanisms and the Management of Health Care: The UK Model and Experience', *International Journal of Public Sector Management*, Vol.7, No.6, pp.15-25 and reprinted in *Journal of Management in Medicine*, Vol.11, No.5, pp.318-328.

Lapsley, I, S Llewellyn and J Grant (1997) *GP Fundholders: Agents of Change*, The Institute of Chartered Accountants of Scotland.

Laurence, J (1991a) 'Freeman Hospital: Countdown to Self-Government', *British Medical Journal*, Vol.302, pp.580-582.

Laurence, J (1991b) 'The Freeman Hospital', *British Medical Journal*, Vol.303, pp.765-766.

Maynard, A (1989) 'Whither the National Health Service?', *The Robbins Lecture*, University of Stirling, 14 November, 1989.

Mohan, J (1990) 'Spatial Implications of the National Health Service White Paper', *Regional Studies*, Vol.24, No.6, pp.553-558.

NHS Executive (1996) *Review of the Trust Financial Regime*, Department of Health.

Packwood, T, J Keen, and M Buxton (1991) *Hospitals in Transition: The Resource Management Experiment*, Open University Press.

Peck, E (1993) 'The Roles of an NHS Trust Board - Aspirations, Observations and Perceptions', pp.62-85, in E Peck and P Spurgeon (eds) *NHS Trusts in Practice*, Longman.

Peck, E (1995) 'The Performance of an NHS Trust Board: Actors' Accounts, Minutes and Observations', *British Journal of Management* Vol.6, pp.135-156.

Perrin, J R (1988) *Resource Management in the NHS*, Van Nostrand Reinhold.

Pettigrew, A (1992) 'On Studying Managerial Elites', *Strategic Management Journal*, Vol.13, pp.163-182.

Propper, C and W Bartlett, (1997) 'The Impact of Competition on the Behaviour of National Health Service Trusts', pp.14-29, in R Flynn and G Williams (eds) *Contracting for Health: Quasi-Markets and the National Health Service*, Oxford University Press.

Sayer, A (1992) *Method in Social Science: A Realist Approach*, 2nd edition, Routledge, London.

Scottish Office (1997) *Designed to Care: Renewing the National Health Service in Scotland*, HMSO, cm 3811, Edinburgh.

Tomkins, C and R Groves (1983) 'The Everyday Accountant and Researching His Reality', *Accounting, Organizations & Society*, Vol.8, No.4, pp.361-374.

APPENDIX A
THEMATIC INTERVIEWS

Executive team

Management processes

- What are the objectives of the Executive/Management Team?
- How are decisions made by the Executive/Management Team? How does it determine priorities, its agenda?
- How do the various professional interests work with the Executive/Management Team?
- Are there sufficiently powerful incentives or penalties for other managers to respond to the directions of the chief executive and the executive?
- How has trust status affected management decision making?
- How has the split between purchaser and provider affected the management of the trust?

Management accounting and financial information systems (MAFIS)

- What are the objectives of MAFIS? How are these met for: capital developments; control of expenditure?
- Any comments on relevance, accuracy, reliability, importance of MAFIS?
- To what extent do members of the Management Team/Executive understand MAFIS? *eg* virement; cash limits; financial targets; budget variances; reserves; options appraisal.
- To what extent does your Management Team/Executive rely on MAFIS for budgetary control?

- To what extent is keeping within the budget more important than delegating responsibility for costs to lower levels of management? In particular, what is the position in clinical areas?
- Has MAFIS facilitated/constrained the contracting process?

Clinical directors

Role

- What do you see as your role within the trust?
- Are you satisfied with it?

Accounting

- What financial information do you receive?
- What do you see as the role of clinical budgeting?

Contracting

- What do you think of the split between purchaser and provider?
- How far are clinicians involved in the contracting process?

Internal environment

- What performance indicators do you use?
- How does responsibility for quality proceed through the hospital process?

Wider issues

- Do you actively monitor events outside the trust which may have a bearing on the trust?
- Do managers use clinicians to understand facets of the market?

Interface between doctor and manager

- Are the medical skills of the staff properly understood by managers in the context of the trusts strategic position?
- Do clinicians have to overcome opposition from managers to implement operational and strategic decisions?

Non executive directors

- Do you contribute to the development of the trust's strategy?
- What kinds of reports and information do you receive? (usefulness?)
- What particular problems does the trust face?
- Are there any clinical or medical issues which are of particular importance at your trust?
- How does the board operate, what is your workload?
- Any comments on the split between purchaser and provider?
- Is there private medical treatment available at this trust?
- Is access to health care a problem for patients at this trust?
- Are there any changes which you would like to see in the operation of the trust or more generally in the organisation of the NHS?